Praise for *Managing People*

"This book beautifully articulates the basic principles of managing people in any field. It highlights the fundamentals every manager needs to master to lead a team effectively. It reminds me of the principles used in baseball's spring training in that every year all of us need to go back to work on the basics to get better—whether we are veterans or rookies. Regardless of your occupation or role in life, this book gives you a how-to guide for managing and great tips for enjoying the journey and your relationships along the way."

    —*Tim Flannery, Third Base Coach, San Francisco Giants Baseball Club*

"This book provides a practical how-to guide for those in leadership and management in any field."

    —*Nicole Jones, President, Jones Enterprises*

"Dean prescribes an understandable, practical means by which organizations can accomplish their mission and managers can effectively execute key initiatives. Further . . . this book can help quickly ramp up new managers and provides a veritable how-to guide for management execution."

    —*Rod Robertson, CEO, Briggs Capital, Inc.*

"This book breaks down management functions in a way for people to be successful right away. It provides good assessment ideas and emphasizes the importance of good communication and mutual understanding. Dean also provides great techniques for coaching, feedback, and conflict resolution. I highly recommend it for all those involved in the field of education."

    —*Gregg Sonken, School Board Member and Principal, Encinitas Union School District*

"This book takes a much-needed approach to the interrelation of the key disciplines of leadership, management, and administration . . . The examples of fictitious companies are helpful in illustrating and applying key techniques and bring the book to life . . . The book is a great tool for managers in any size company."

    —*Scott Wilcox, CEO, The W Group*

Managing People

Processes, Strategies, and Tools
for Leaders and Managers in Every Field

Dean Sickels

Cultiver Group Publishing Company
Carlsbad, CA

Cultiver Group Publishing Company
800 Grand Avenue, Suite A-11
Carlsbad, CA 92008
www.CultiverGroup.com

Rolling Agendas is a trademark of the Cultiver Group.

Ordering Information

Quantity sales. Special discounts are available on quantity purchases by corporations, associations, and others. For details, contact the "Special Sales Department" at the address above.

Individual sales. Cultiver Group Publishing Company publications are available through most bookstores. They can also be ordered directly from BCH: Tel: (800) 431-1579; Fax: (914) 835-0398; www.bookch.com.

Orders by US trade bookstores and wholesalers. Please contact BCH: Tel: (800) 431-1579; Fax: (914) 835-0398; www.bookch.com.

Cataloging-in-Publication
Sickels, Dean.
   Managing people : processes, strategies, and tools for
leaders and managers in every field / Dean Sickels --
1st ed.
   p. cm.
   Includes index.
   LCCN 2011926860
   ISBN-13: 978-0-9834779-2-1

   1. Management. 2. Leadership.   I. Title.

HD57.7.S53 2011   658.4'092
                         QBI11-600151

Printed in the United States of America

First Edition

16 15 14 13 12 11   10 9 8 7 6 5 4 3 2 1

Cover design: Kuo Designs
Interior design: Marin Bookworks
Copyediting: PeopleSpeak

This book is dedicated to my parents for the foundation they gave me and their never-ending encouragement to our family.

Table of Contents

Acknowledgments

I would like to thank my wonderful wife and friend, Sydney, and our great kids, Erin, Kevin, and Robin.

I would also like to thank the many terrific teachers, mentors, and colleagues I have learned from over the years, including Wally, Doe, Randy, Pat, Martin, Rick, PD, Billie, Bill, Rudy, Mike, Dick, Terry, Peter, JP, Tim, Denis, Craig, Shawn, Andre, Chris, Daryl, Deron, Dave, and JC. Thanks to EBGB for her contributions.

Introduction

ALL OF US are leaders and managers in life. We lead and manage in a variety of roles, including those of parent, teacher, business-person, volunteer coordinator, and virtually any other position you can think of. We are all leaders because we influence one another. We are all managers because we supervise our time, schedules, and resources in a variety of ways.

In over two decades of management experience in a variety of fields including technology, education, and ministry, I have confirmed that the same basic principles apply to successfully leading and managing people in any field. This book highlights the critical principles needed to lead, manage, and administer competently across all disciplines. It is intended to be a practical how-to guide to help managers do their jobs effectively, not another book of theories about leadership.

The book suggests ideas, concepts, and practical tools for all levels of management. It can serve as both a review for seasoned leaders and a guide for those who are new in leadership and management positions. New managers need direction and suggestions so they can develop their own unique leadership styles and be productive right from the start. Ironically, organizations spend so much time training people in specific content and so little time training them in how to execute the day-to-day tasks of their jobs. As a result, most of us are ill equipped to lead, manage, and administer adequately in our initial roles.

This book is divided into three parts: "Leadership," "Management," and "Administration." These three disciplines are very different, but they are also intimately interrelated. Leaders must understand all three to accomplish the mission and goals of their organization and be effective in their roles.

Part 1 discusses the fundamental skills leaders need and the personal qualities they must develop to be successful as leaders. Leadership is not a person's position, title, designation, and status although these may help get a group's attention. Plaques, trophies, and certificates don't make a leader either. Someone can have incredible abilities in certain areas but not have leadership qualities. Leaders are people who can influence, motivate, and inspire a group to strive for the fulfillment of a mission and goals. They can stimulate a sustained effort and provide vision for the team to accomplish great things.

Part 2 offers management strategies that will streamline your job as a manager. Management is the ability to direct people skillfully and to succeed in accomplishing a goal. Managers need to fully understand the organization's priorities so they can set goals, make plans, and develop tasks to accomplish the organization's mission. To do this, managers need to know how to organize, delegate, make decisions, and develop successful teams. For that they need both tactical skills and interpersonal skills.

Part 3 covers the key administrative tools, techniques, and skills needed for success. Administration applies leadership skills and management skills to the day-to-day routine. You'll learn how to create job descriptions, recruit and interview new people, and bring them on board smoothly. You'll also find out how to create an information base for your organization and make sure the word gets out about what sets your organization apart.

Throughout the book you'll find practical techniques you can use immediately in your job. One great tool is the rolling agenda, which will help you juggle many tasks, organize your team, and stay focused on accomplishing the organization's mission.

To help you see how to apply these tools and techniques in a variety of organizations, the book uses case studies and examples from several fictitious companies, particularly the LGLO Specialty Shoe Store and the Acme School District. A "Quick Reference" section at the end of every chapter puts the main points of the chapter at your fingertips.

Whether you are a leader in business, education, construction, ministry, volunteer coordination, your home, or another field, you'll find common elements to managing people and tasks. My hope is that this book will help ease the transition for new leaders and help sharpen the skills of veteran leaders by providing proven ideas and concepts and a framework to improve your performance.

PART I

Leadership

B Y DEFINITION, LEADERSHIP is the ability to show the way by going along with or being in front of another individual. The first part of this definition can be at odds with perceptions that leaders are separated from other people. Coming alongside people to lead them can be a bit of a foreign concept. Most leaders try to lead from the front, but if they look back and no one is following, then they should probably reassess their effectiveness.

Good leaders have the ability to influence people in one-on-one conversations and in groups, large or small. In both cases you need good motivational skills to be successful. One-to-one leadership assumes a partnership involving two people who are jointly motivated to accomplish a specific initiative or goal. One-to-many leadership requires the expertise to inspire a group to individually and collectively adopt a vision to fulfill an organization's mission, goals, and plans.

Leadership competence is both innate and learned. People may be born with certain leadership characteristics and qualities, but leadership is developed and refined every day through awareness, perseverance, and self-discipline. You must continually build on the skills you have learned and apply them to new situations and circumstances. You need to be a dedicated, lifelong learner who is attuned to what you can learn and how to apply it.

Leadership styles can differ dramatically, but effectiveness is always measured in results and outcomes. Style is a function of a leader's personality, belief system, makeup, and experiences. For example, General George Patton had a drastically different leadership approach from that of Mother Teresa, but both people were incredibly successful at accomplishing their missions and goals.

Your leadership style must match your personality or it can seem contrived. This means you have to know yourself in order to have an effective leadership style.

In addition, the head of any group has to realize just how important peer leadership is to attain a desired outcome. What is said when you are absent from the group is just as important as what is said when you are present. You need to ensure that peer leaders offer positive messaging and reinforce key objectives within the team. Negative messaging and influence by peer leaders will torpedo any initiative or at least limit group effort and effectiveness. Key peer influencers are referred to by a variety of terms including "captain," "right hand," and "go-to person." Peer leadership is absolutely critical to achieving the goals of the leader and the organization.

Another vital factor to recognize is that successful leaders sacrifice a tremendous amount in their lives. Heading any group can be frustrating and very tiring. A common idea is that leaders are self-centered, but this is far from true. The more responsibility with which leaders are entrusted, the more they are required to give up. Rather than being self-centered, successful leaders are always looking out for the good of the organization, and they must continually make sacrifices. In the same way, teamwork also requires individual sacrifice. At some point, each individual on a team will have to sacrifice his or her own near-term goal or agenda for the good of the team. Sacrifice is not a one-time deed; it is a set of constant, exemplary acts. Sacrifice is an ongoing behavior that sets a great example for all people and in turn develops tremendous personal character.

Although leadership is sometimes exhausting, there is no greater feeling than having guided a team to fulfill significant goals. To help you achieve this, the next three chapters will focus on the requisite building blocks of leadership. These leadership fundamentals are not meant to be definitive doctrine, but rather concepts you can use to examine and improve your overall leadership.

CHAPTER 1

Mastering the Intangible Factors of Leadership

S OLID LEADERSHIP DOESN'T just happen. It is developed by establishing the foundational necessities and building on them. This chapter examines a few of the intangible qualities necessary for leadership: trust, communication, respect, people skills, experience, credibility, relationships, strategic thinking, vision, momentum, and consensus building. You'll also have an opportunity to assess your own areas of strength and areas that need improvement.

Trust

Trust is a crucial ingredient of competent leadership. It is earned by doing what you say, communicating effectively, and producing positive results with both individuals and the organization at large. Being a leader can come with a great deal of scrutiny and potential criticism. To gain people's trust, you must show competence for the subject matter you oversee, and you must connect to group members individually and collectively while stressing partnership.

Trust is also earned and reinforced by a leader's character. Character is often defined as the way people behave when no one is watching. This is contrasted with personality, which is defined as the way people behave when around other people. Leaders who consistently show character through right behavior can engender trust. People are attracted to individuals of high character, which enables these individuals to lead for extensive periods.

Integrity is also an important component in building trust. It requires honest communication with individuals and groups. Nothing is more demoralizing to people than when they sense they are being lied to or manipulated. They will quickly begin to distrust the leader, thus hindering the organization's efforts.

The only way to truly build trust is by working in partnership with people to achieve common goals, expectations, and results. You have to take people's individual goals into consideration and help accomplish them as well. You cannot build trust by simply talking about it. Trust has to be developed by people together on the basis of mutual respect.

Communication

Building trust requires clear communication that consists of frequent streams of interaction and completed conversations. Completed conversations are interactions that end with both parties having their questions answered and a better understanding of each other's intentions and decision-making processes.

Take a moment to evaluate your own style of communication. Do you avoid organizational jargon? Do you discuss expected learning curves with individuals? Do you avoid micromanaging details? Do you highlight priorities so your team knows what's important? Do you regularly ask team members questions that gauge their understanding?

Leaders often forget to communicate a key point or do not articulate a task or plan in detail the first time it is discussed. This can lead to an incomplete conversation in which expectations and tasks are unclear. Never expect comprehensive understanding if a message is offered only once. You may have thought out your ideas completely, with careful attention and in painstaking detail. However, when you communicate these ideas, you may neglect to explain them with the same thoroughness. You may think you have conveyed a clear message, but your team members may be confused and may initiate a project or task with a limited understanding. This can impair an activity from the beginning. When the team returns to you with an assignment that misses the mark, you may criticize them for not doing the task as you had outlined it when the real problem is that the task was not communicated properly. Missed expectations like these can lead to a sense of distrust.

A completed conversation—whether in person, via telephone, by e-mail, or by text—is the responsibility of both parties. That is, both parties are obligated to complete the conversation and confirm expectations. Good leaders consistently communicate by using a steady stream of questions and confirmations to ensure that individuals and teams have a clear understanding of what is expected. When you relate expectations repeatedly and specifically, effective communication can take place.

When you complete conversations and your communication is clear, expectations have a greater chance of being met. And when expectations are met, mutual trust develops along with a good working relationship that will enable you to create momentum.

Respect

Respect, like trust, is an intangible necessity for a leader. Some leaders say, "My people don't have to like me, but they have to respect me." This is true, but you still have to establish a relationship for mutual respect to develop. The ability to achieve a goal is sustainable only for a short period of time if respect and trust are not developed. Ironically, respect is most often exhibited when a leader is absent—in conversations among individuals on the team. And just as gossip has a negative impact, positive peer conversations can have a positive impact.

Respect develops over time as you make the right decisions and you relate to people in a professional and empathetic manner. It also comes from admitting mistakes when your decisions don't turn out for the best and acknowledging when you don't know something. Showing a consistent, positive attitude can also set you apart and lead to gaining respect. Your calmness and proficiency in dealing with challenges and difficult situations are vital to developing respect. Quick situation analysis and problem resolution are also factors in growing respect and trust.

We are all familiar with the grumbling, gossiping, and second-guessing sometimes aimed at those in high-level decision-making positions. You need to rise above the negativity, stay focused, and direct your team toward the goal.

If you get in the habit of always making decisions in the best interest of the organization and not in your own interest, respect will come your way. Should you have disagreements about a plan with someone in a decision-making capacity, approach him or her in a one-on-one meeting to share your thoughts and glean additional information. You may then offer help, input, potential solutions, or alternative opinions, and in turn you will advance your understanding of the situation.

Leaders make decisions and enact plans based on the big picture of what they are trying to accomplish. By framing and communicating your plan in that context, you will enable your team to see elements that they may have not considered when formulating their initial opinions. Good leaders will often amend or adjust a plan based on relevant input from others. Whatever the outcome of such encounters, you should be willing to implement the final decision and put your personal feelings or agenda behind you. This behavior will always contribute to the building of respect.

People Skills

The most critical resource of any organization is its people. In most organizations, people represent the largest part of the budget and resource pool. As a leader, you need to view each individual as crucial to your collective success, not as a project, number, or necessity. The development and mentorship of your people should be your greatest fulfillment and ultimate legacy. Do you spend the requisite amount of time developing your human resources, or are you too busy? Do you hastily give out directives and expect people to accomplish them without the proper amount of communication and training?

Enjoy the companionship of your team. Otherwise, your labors will be mostly in vain and your achievements hollow. We all have a great need for relationships. Realize this need in yourself and coworkers, and take the time to fulfill it. Treat your coworkers with the respect they deserve and as the individuals they are. Partner with them to carry out common objectives and enjoy your mutual success when you execute a plan and achieve your goals.

In the end, most of us will value the relationships we have developed during our workdays much more than the accolades, recognition, or money we have received. A common saying is that people on their deathbeds never wish they had spent more time at work or making more money. Instead, they wish they had spent more time developing relationships with family, friends, and coworkers.

Spending one-on-one time with people shows you value them and their labor. Remember to engage them as human beings rather than employees. Relax occasionally and have some fun. It won't compromise your leadership standing to act human.

You may get frustrated when goals are not being met quickly enough, which can lead to demoralizing conversations with your team members. To avoid this pitfall, think of the ramifications of your words before you speak. Before you blame others, look at your own responsibility. Have you done more than simply direct people? Have you taught, developed, come alongside, and served them to help accomplish your mutual objectives? Has your own ambition blinded you to others' needs, or do you have compassion and empathy for the situations people are going through? Only by showing a willingness to connect with people individually can you develop their trust.

Your people skills are vital to your ability to lead. Fundamentally, there are two ways to lead. You can lift others up emotionally through encouragement or you can lift yourself up by putting others down. Most people respond positively to encouragement, and the resultant motivation will raise their performance. That is not to say that communication should always be flowery. Good leaders hold their team members accountable, but that does not mean that berating them is an effective way to motivate them.

When holding a person accountable and giving feedback on his or her performance, use the "sandwich" principle. Start your communication with something positive about the person, then describe the performance area that needs improvement. Make the critique as specific and measurable as possible. End with a positive statement, and make sure that you gain agreement on the person's area of improvement and strengths. Here's an example from the Acme School District, a fictitious organization used for examples throughout this book.

A new principal named Greg was doing a good job, but he was neglecting to inspect weekly lesson plans. This task was vital to make sure teachers were executing the school district's standards and methodologies. The superintendent, Joyce, addressed the situation with

Greg in a sandwich conversation: "Greg, you're a great addition to our administrative staff, and you've already developed great respect from both the district and your peers in a short amount of time. You are really advancing our mission and achieving our goals. One area we would like you to focus on a bit more is the inspection of lesson plans. The inspection is critical because we need our teachers to plan and teach according to the agreed-upon district standards and methodologies. Greg, how do you think you're doing in that area, and how can you work this task into your schedule?"

At this point the superintendent needed to get Greg to acknowledge the performance area that needed improvement and buy into its importance. Once Greg had done this, Joyce could conclude the conversation: "Greg, thanks for acknowledging the importance of the lesson planning process and prioritizing it on your schedule. Let's meet in two weeks to review your progress in this area. Thanks again for all your hard work and your dedication to the students and teachers. You are a great addition to the Acme School District."

Notice how the superintendent started with a positive statement, related the needed area of improvement, and then ended with a positive statement.

Like a real sandwich, the focus in a sandwich conversation is on the meat in the middle. If people cannot understand that an area of performance needs improvement, they will not make meaningful progress in that area even if you feel that you have communicated it thoroughly. However, unless you frame the conversation properly at the beginning and end, you cannot lead the discussion effectively.

Leaders who consistently put others down will be effective only for a short time because the team's motivation will not be sustained. Intimidating people and placing them under undue negative stress will take a toll on them emotionally. Eventually they won't be motivated to do a good job, or they will seek employment or service elsewhere.

Putting others down repeatedly is characteristic of leaders who are insecure. Leaders who use encouragement are more self-assured. Those who build others up around them can sustain motivation for long periods. When a key goal is accomplished, a leader can increase the entire team's motivation by giving others credit. After all, the leader may have established the strategic elements of the plan, but the team members are the ones who executed the tasks to achieve the desired results. Recognizing individual team members and the group as a whole reflects a selfless attitude by the leader and is great for promoting team bonding and creating momentum.

There is no substitute for good people skills. All people are created and motivated differently, and part of your job is to help unlock everyone's potential.

Experience

Experience is a vital asset in leading and dealing with the multiplicity of decision-making situations that arise in any organization. Lessons learned and past successes and failures form your educational foundation and should help shape good decision making as you encounter similar situations in the future. No matter how painful they may seem at the time, all experiences can be used and shared with others to help them in their work or personal lives. Experiences can be extremely helpful if you can effectively apply the lessons learned. Sharing them can also make you more credible as a leader.

Young leaders face a challenge because they may not have yet encountered a lot of situations, circumstances, or conditions on which to base their decisions. This is not, by any means, an insurmountable obstacle. Young leaders should be more deliberate in their decision-making process. They should seek out leaders whom they respect and pick their brains for strategic, tactical, and operational ideas. These suggestions can greatly improve young leaders' learning curves and enable them to absorb valuable experiences.

Credibility

When you have credibility, people believe in you and your ability to do something. Credibility is an intangible that can be difficult to achieve. It is usually earned with a pattern of successes. Without credibility, a leader will find it almost impossible to accomplish anything. Credibility grows when a leader makes good decisions and team members recognize and validate those decisions. It is often established when the leader is not present, and it surfaces in conversations among team members. You can't really talk about your credibility yourself; rather, it is established by those around you. If you show the necessary leadership qualities and are successful in decision making and problem solving, you will establish credibility. Although your credibility can be established by what others say about you, it still needs to be cemented by your actions.

Relationships

Relationships are the focal point of all organizations, just as they are the key in our personal lives. People work better when they connect with one another and get along. Positive relationships lead to the creation of a healthy environment, which in turn helps the organization fulfill its objectives. People who are isolated contribute to negative environments, and negative results usually occur. They watch the clock and count the minutes until it is time to go home.

In a healthy environment, productivity is greatly increased and people are motivated to go the extra mile for the team and organization. You need to constantly monitor the environment and make the proper adjustments to ensure it is positive.

You must also strive to create an environment where good relationships can develop. Relationships typically don't "just happen." They are intentional, and you are responsible for facilitating and fostering them. It is said that "people don't care how much you know until they know how much you care." This idea is foundational in creating an environment for developing productive relationships. This book places a tremendous emphasis on relationships because they are vital to leadership.

Strategic Thinking

Regardless of the situation, effective leaders must always keep track of the big picture: the mission and goals of the organization. They must execute key initiatives and tasks while always keeping in mind the organization's overall strategic direction.

To think strategically, you need to be in a continual state of evaluation and adjustment. The organization's mission typically will not change dramatically, but adjustments in your strategies should be commonplace. Very rarely does a plan work sufficiently the way it is originally written. In addition, the goals and priorities involved in achieving the mission will change as external and internal conditions change. The ability to adjust while keeping the mission as a priority is critical for good leaders.

Part of strategic thinking is providing direction and motivation to your team. Motivating people has to be a strategic underpinning to everything you do.

Great leaders are constantly thinking strategically about how they will achieve the mission and how they will motivate their people to achieve it. If the leaders of an organization dream big, they have to put the people, processes, and systems in place to achieve the dream. The only way to scale resources properly is to provide consistent empowerment, communication, and course adjustment to team members. This is something that is done not once but continually in small and large ways. Leaders walk a fine line between micromanaging, and giving team members the proper space to achieve results and experience the fulfillment of their efforts.

Strategic thought should include a succession plan for key leaders. No single person can build and sustain success over a long period of time. Personality-based organizations that focus on a single leader will eventually fail. Organizations that have been successful over time have a solid depth and breadth of executive leadership. This depth should be mirrored throughout an organization so that leaders are always available who can be raised up and called on when necessary. Otherwise, the organization will experience large gaps during which goals are compromised and growth diminishes.

The leader's job is to strategically build the organization, systems, processes, people, and development structure to achieve great growth that will outlast the leader. Every leader will eventually leave an organization through some type of circumstance, be it a job change, promotion, retirement, or death. Good organizations have developed a system in which leaders can leave and others can step in to take their place with a minimum amount of disruption or decrease in productivity.

Strategic leaders see their legacy as the ability to raise up people around them who could potentially take their position. To be successful, this approach takes leaders of strong character, without large egos. Such leaders must be committed to their organization's mission and put its goals above themselves. If an organization is able to build this approach into its culture, it will seldom experience declines or gaps, and it can sustain consistent growth.

Vision

Leaders must have vision, the ability to see and anticipate the future before others in the organization. As the Bible says, "Where there is no vision, the people perish." Leaders must see the desired result far in advance and be able to communicate it to the members of the organization in a tangible way. The vision includes both the end goal and the road markers that will indicate whether the organization is on track.

As a leader you have to apply your experience and anticipate challenges and obstacles before they occur. In addition, you must be able to formulate solutions and plans as soon as problems arise. With appropriate anticipation, challenges can be overcome quickly. Of course, it is better if obstacles never materialize, but at least you can have the vision to work through the desired response mentally and emotionally.

As milestones are accomplished, stay ahead of the team and its goals by projecting the vision forward. Always anticipate and keep the mission in the forefront as a guidepost to the tasks that need to be realized. Vision and anticipation are difficult to teach; they are usually developed through experience, awareness, and intuition. Therefore, you need to practice developing vision in daily situations. This will help you cultivate the skill and apply it to larger plans and challenges.

Momentum

Creating and sustaining momentum is another intangible part of leadership. Momentum is most apparent when all members of the team are contributing and attaining good results simultaneously and sequentially. Momentum can be defined as a series of little things going right. It provides the foundation for larger and larger initiatives and dreams to be accomplished. When an organization is working on a goal or project and starts completing tasks, the group can get "on a roll." A key factor in building momentum is the confidence that results from executing tasks and reaching goals; confidence removes real or perceived roadblocks. You need to constantly stoke the fire and direct and encourage team members. To sustain momentum, anticipate organizational needs, make proper adjustments, and stay 90 to 180 days or more ahead of the team.

Without momentum, no results will be achieved, no problems solved, and no change created. Only a series of starts and stops will occur. Momentum is essential to the long-term health of an organization. With enough momentum, planning, and competence, anything can be achieved. A good leader understands this and can manage the ebb and flow and take advantage of the positive energy that momentum can bring to an organization. When you create an environment in which people can be successful and tasks can be accomplished, momentum will be a natural result. Great goals can be accomplished, negative trends can be reversed, and great change can happen if you understand the vital nature of momentum.

Consensus Building

There is no such thing as group buy-in; there is only individual buy-in and collective ownership. Consensus is developed through the sometimes arduous process of gathering input about how a goal can be accomplished. In this process, all affected individuals need to have input on the plan, addressing the elements of who, what, when, where, why, and how. As laborious as the process may be, don't take shortcuts in consensus building. This form of collaboration will lay the foundation for the execution of key initiatives.

Note that certain parts of the plan will not be negotiable. You need to set the what and why elements of the plan and explain how they relate to the overall mission and goals of the organization. Then you can build consensus and gather input about the who, when, where, and how parts of the plan.

Consensus building in a collaborative model is not easy, and you should anticipate potential opposition and prolonged dialogue before resolution is reached. In societies today, adversarial communication is much more common than collaboration. This trend can be attributed to the litigious manner in which our disagreements are often resolved and the accompanying culture that has developed. When building consensus, think through every aspect of and potential problem with a specific plan prior to presenting the plan for input. By anticipating objections, you can formulate proper responses and easily deliver them in group or one-on-one discussions. (If you don't meet opposition or confrontation, consider yourself fortunate.)

The consensus-building process will bring out fresh ideas that can be implemented in the ultimate strategic goal and plan. It can uncover beneficial insights from people who are more familiar with the intricacies of specific situations and problems.

Consensus building is best done in one-on-one or small group meetings so as to defuse any potential negative group dynamics. These meetings can be labeled "brainstorming sessions" because this name implies that no idea or suggestion will necessarily be implemented. (See chapter 6 for effective techniques for brainstorming sessions.) By seeking input and building consensus among individuals, you will create momentum when the ultimate plan or solution is devised and presented to the group. The unhealthiest environment for a group occurs when individuals sit in silence while their leader proposes a plan created without proper input. Lack of input will most likely lead to a lack of detail, which will result in poor energy and momentum when the plan is launched.

Quick Reference

Good leadership is built on a foundation of intangible qualities. Many of these, such as respect and credibility, are established not by you but by what is said about you within the group when you are not present.

Trust

- You build trust by showing competence in your field and communicating effectively.
- Your character and integrity will help earn the trust of your team.
- Trust grows out of mutual respect.

Communication

- Communication needs to be clear, frequent, and easily understood.
- Completed conversations result in better mutual understanding.

- You can't expect good results if you don't communicate a task in detail.

Respect

- You gain respect over time by making the right decisions and by admitting mistakes when necessary.
- Respect comes from your calm proficiency in dealing with challenges and difficult situations.
- You need to be willing to put your personal feelings or agenda behind you.
- Building consensus builds respect.

People Skills

- People are the most critical resource of any organization, and your job is to help people unlock their potential.
- You should try to enjoy your relationships with the people on your team.
- You need to treat your coworkers with the respect they deserve and as the individuals they are.
- Effective leaders practice the sandwich principle: When giving someone feedback on his or her performance, start the communication with a positive statement. Then communicate the performance area that needs improvement. Finally, end with something positive.

Experience

- Experience is helpful only if you apply the lessons you learned.
- Young leaders who lack experience need to be more careful in making decisions and find mentors who can improve their learning curve.

Credibility

- Credibility is usually earned with a pattern of successes.
- You can't talk about your own credibility. It's established by those around you, but you need to reinforce it with your actions.

Relationships

- People work better when they connect with one another and get along.
- You are responsible for creating an environment that facilitates and fosters relationships.

Strategic Thinking

- You must always keep track of the big picture and keep your team motivated.
- Great leaders are committed to their organization's mission and put its goals above themselves.
- You need to build a succession plan for key leaders because no single person can build and sustain success over a long period of time.

Vision

- Leaders must be able to anticipate events far in advance and communicate their vision to their team.
- You need to anticipate challenges and obstacles before they arise and formulate potential solutions.

Momentum

- Momentum is attained when everyone on the team is getting good results.
- Instilling confidence among the team members will create momentum.
- If you create an environment in which tasks can be successfully accomplished, momentum will result.

Consensus Building

- Consensus building requires gathering input that will bring out new ideas.
- The what and why elements of a plan are usually not negotiable, but you should build consensus for who, when, where, and how.

- Calling consensus-building meetings "brainstorming sessions" implies that no idea will necessarily be implemented.
- When you build consensus, you create momentum for the plan that will ultimately be launched.

CHAPTER 2

Developing Personal Leadership Qualities

I N ADDITION TO the intangible leadership factors examined in chapter 1, leaders need to develop a host of personal leadership qual ities to be successful. This chapter will examine some of those qualities.

Setting the Example

Good leaders must set an example for all the behaviors they desire from their team. There is no such thing as "Do as I say, not as I do." People learn more from observing consistent behavior than they will ever learn from what someone says to them. Leaders have to rise above controversies, jealousies, gossip, and personal attacks to accomplish the organization's mission and goals.

Leaders also have to diligently set an example by admitting their mistakes. This will allow others to take risks to achieve goals and not be thwarted by their own mistakes. Like their leader, team members have to learn from their mistakes and successes and move forward by building on those experiences.

Pointing out individual mistakes while still promoting learning and maintaining team and individual motivation is an art. You have to walk a fine line when you correct mistakes made by team members.

Continually referring to past failures does no good because it discourages people and decreases their motivation.

Begin the learning process by describing the mistake in specific terms. Make sure the person takes ownership of the mistake. Then together, look at other potential actions that might have led to a better outcome.

Pointing out a mistake and advancing the learning process is very similar to using the sandwich principle referred to in chapter 1. You are attempting to frame the mistake in context, have the person acknowledge it, and help prevent similar mistakes in the future. To illustrate, we'll go back to our fictitious Principal Greg in the Acme School District. Greg approved a field trip using parent volunteers as drivers. Two of the drivers got lost, leading to a series of events that could have been avoided.

Here's how Superintendent Joyce discussed the situation with Greg: "Greg, I heard that the field trip didn't go so well yesterday. I applaud you for wanting the kids to have experiences outside of school and connect with the community. You're not the first person to have a bad incident with volunteer drivers. In the future, I think it would be wise if we either have teachers drive or have a fund-raiser to help us offset the cost of a bus. Sound good? I don't want to discourage you from field trips because they are an important part of our community connection goal. The field trips for which we rented buses were great. Thanks for prioritizing this goal; you're doing a nice job connecting our kids to the community."

In the example, the superintendent started with a factual statement, addressed the mistake, and then ended with a positive comment. She avoided being too negative. Too much focus on mistakes will cause people to become risk averse and not strive to reach their full potential in the future. If they begin to play it too safe, their results will be mediocre.

When leaders reach out to their people and come alongside them to help, they set a great example and develop bonds that can greatly improve overall teamwork. Remember, the definition of leadership is the ability to show the way by going along with or in front of another. A common bond increases motivation exponentially as you and team members work together to attain a mutual objective. By coming alongside and assisting people, you are demonstrating that you value them and want to help them fulfill their responsibilities.

You have to constantly remember that you are being watched and assessed for positive and negative behaviors. Positive behavior is both caught and taught. You are held to different standards than the individuals you manage. So, when you show frustration with team members and feel a sense of negativity set in, it may be wise to withdraw and regroup before you say or do something you may regret. On the other hand, allowing team members to see a small amount of frustration is healthy because it will keep them attuned to the need for performance improvement and reinforce high expectations. But witnessing a major blowup or being repeatedly exposed to this type of behavior can significantly demotivate people. Discouragement and lack of motivation will result in reduced performance and ultimately can lead to turnover.

Self-Assessment

As leaders we spend so much time focused on the individuals we manage that we can neglect to spend the necessary time to assess our own performance. We need to develop the ability to honestly and objectively assess our personal strengths and weaknesses. None of us are perfect. We need to actively use our strengths to develop others and seek ways to improve in the areas where we are lacking. We can also supplement our areas of known weakness with people who are strong in them. Knowing our strengths and weaknesses is critical in leadership.

At times, publicly acknowledging your weaknesses and areas where you need development is a good idea. It will model the behavior you want your team to follow. Leaders must be willing to potentially look foolish by taking small and large risks to accomplish great feats. Think of the many great leaders who have taken great risks or of those who had physical, emotional, or intellectual impediments and have overcome them because of their passionate commitment to their causes.

In addition to seeking improvement in your weakness areas, you need to accentuate and fully utilize your areas of strength. Your greatest impact on others will come when you share and direct your team members in your strength areas. You will also minimize your personal stress by working in those areas. Your ability to accomplish great things will most likely be realized by focusing on your strengths.

Despite the fact that you have been put in a position of leadership, an air of superiority or self-importance turns people off quickly, and it can make your job tougher. Your job is to teach, motivate, cajole, and develop your team to achieve the mission of the organization, not your own agenda. However, you need to keep an arm's length between you and those you manage so you can deal with potential issues in an objective manner. Everyone wants to be liked, but without some separation you will be viewed as a peer and your effectiveness will be limited. A lack of this type of separation is a common problem with those who are in leadership or management for the first time or who have risen to leadership from a peer position.

All of these areas of performance, along with the more specific elements of your position, need to be integrated into your self-assessment to maximize your strengths and enable you to create a specific development plan. We are never too experienced to learn or improve ourselves. Great leaders are lifelong learners.

Awareness

Leaders must develop an awareness to see more in depth than others, see farther than others, assess circumstances, formulate actions, and enact plans that address challenges and situations in a timely manner. They must examine conditions in detail and consider projections of the future—striking a balance between optimism, facts, and reality—before they can set a realistic plan and communicate it to the team for implementation. Good leaders constantly run situations through their minds to look at potential risk and reward scenarios.

Don't get stuck in the box; rather, apply original thoughts and imagination to find the best possible solution to a challenge. Be aware of all variables and input and don't take shortcuts. Good leaders love the exercise of putting together a puzzle in their mind before enacting a plan.

In new situations where you have limited experience, listen to others intently and absorb as much as possible, much like you did in your first job. Targeted, open-ended questions can help you learn about a particular subject. Consult a variety of resources internal and external to your organization to assess all angles of a situation. When you prepare by reading and accessing available resources, you will broaden your awareness and shorten your learning curve.

Developing an awareness of what your team members need and when they need it is also a key element of leadership. Great leaders have great timing. Oftentimes, *when* you say something is just as important as *what* you say. People receive only a limited amount of content in the communication process, so how and when you say something is critical to motivation and understanding. Good leaders realize that they will experience an assortment of ups and downs. Great leaders will tell you that the way to develop a consistent, long-term pattern of success is to stay on an even keel and maintain an awareness of the big picture.

Most new leaders and managers make the mistake of becoming overly confident. They may loosen up when events are going well. Conversely, they may become overly negative, critical, and demanding when events are not going as planned. Great coaches will tell you that you should do exactly the opposite. When things are going well, tighten the screws and make sure the team is not getting lackadaisical or complacent. Make sure you don't stop stressing the urgency needed to execute the plans you have implemented to attain your goals.

Alternatively, when events are going poorly, be aware that people need encouragement to reestablish their confidence. Reinforce the goal or plan, make any necessary adjustments, and reassure the team that the goal will be accomplished. When you reestablish confidence, you can regain momentum. You don't ever want a team to become resigned to failure and experience the subsequent performance drop-off that occurs if confidence erodes.

Having an awareness of your individual team members' motivational needs and the collective team need is more art than science. Keeping your eyes and ears open will help you develop an awareness as to what is required and when it should be addressed.

Emotional Strength

You have to constantly motivate individuals or groups to achieve a plan or goal. Even the most logical plan will never be attained unless you can influence someone to emotionally buy into it and execute it. The brain may process and accept a plan, but it takes both the head and heart to make it happen. Having emotional strength is vital to sustaining motivation and enables your team to achieve the organization's mission and goals.

Your ability to face a problem or challenge and devise a solution without getting overwhelmed is a crucial form of emotional strength. This involves finding a way to emotionally minimize the challenges by keeping them in perspective. Very few stressful situations are really a matter of life and death. In fact, when it looks like everything is caving in or falling apart, you may want to use humor to break the tension and ensure rational thinking to handle the situation. A phrase like "We have them just where we want them!" is great for perspective. A little humor can go a long way toward framing the situation properly, neutralizing the negative stress, and enabling you to enact the proper plan to address the circumstances.

If you can personally look at a trial as an exciting challenge instead of reacting with fear or anxiety, you can communicate the solution or plan with confidence and immediately set the team on a productive course. When you embrace the situations that test you, you develop character and emotional strength.

In some circumstances, you may have to devise solutions quickly, which can tax everyone's emotions. Your initial plan or solution may not be 100 percent correct, but it will set the team on a path to resolution and provide a direction forward. It is wise to present the solution boldly. You can always make adjustments later to tweak your solution and target it more closely to the goal. Quickly moving forward gets emotions going in the right direction as well.

Another key emotional strength is to be self-assured in who you are and in your position within the organization. This will enable you to recruit, hire, develop, and surround yourself with the best possible people. Self-assuredness confirms that you are confident enough in your abilities that you do not see talented people as a threat to your position or standing in the organization. If you focus on the organization's goals and execute actions to achieve them, your personal goals will follow.

All ventures will have inflection points where the heat is turned up and the pressure is applied to individuals and groups. Their occurrence can be attributed to high expectations, accelerated time lines, unforeseen challenges, or a host of other issues. This is when exceptional leaders are at their best. They will set the emotional tone for how to deal with the situation because they know that if the leader panics, the team will respond in kind. If the leader exhibits calmness, assesses the situation,

creates the appropriate sense of urgency, and then sets the team or organization on a well-thought-out course, team members typically follow
the leader's example. This will enable the team to take the pressure and
nervousness of a situation and turn it into positive energy, accept the
challenge, and ultimately execute the desired plan. Leaders always need
to show calm on the outside, even though they may be churning on the
inside, just like a duck looks as if it is gliding on top of the water but is
paddling like crazy under it. Calm in the face of adversity is the sign of
an exceptional leader, one who has developed emotional strength.

Discipline

People are always watching to see if you are going to take a shortcut
because your self-discipline will set the tone for the project, initiative,
and team. Consistency in your daily activities reinforces your leadership
behavior and projects discipline. The self-discipline to power through
obstacles and sometimes mundane tasks is a quality others look up to.
Some facets of leadership are not very glamorous, but self-discipline in
the daily grind will earn you a lot of respect. Doing tasks you don't want
to do without complaint is a form of self-discipline. It is said that you
can't get much done in life if you only work on the days you feel good.
This reflects the consistency that is required to be an effective leader.

Preparation is a discipline that sets apart any individual in any
endeavor. In fast-paced, always-connected cultures, we get used to taking care of the immediate and many times don't allocate the requisite
time to plan and do something right the first time. However, every small
or large task requires the discipline of preparation. Good leaders will
spend extra time in preparation for key activities. The effort involved
in creating well-organized plans or meetings is readily apparent to all
participants. Discipline in preparation shows people you care about the
subject matter and them. Conversely, shoddy preparation devalues an
activity in the minds of the participants. Poor discipline will discredit a
leader more than any other quality.

Will and Focus

Will is another key personal quality leaders have to apply to all situations, large or small. It is the ability to project success before a task is
undertaken. Most people have to be taught how to consistently think

they will succeed at what they are trying to accomplish. They have to be motivated and focused on the tangible duties that are required to win. Like momentum, will is made possible when a series of small events has a positive outcome and team members realize that goals are being achieved. Confidence builds and collective will is easier to sustain.

You must set the tone by expressing without any hesitation or doubt that an initiative will be realized. Although team members may question their capacity to fulfill big dreams until they see results, you must project a strong will and help them visualize the successful completion of a goal before it is realized.

Focus your team on goals and objectives and emphatically communicate the plan to execute them. It is impossible to lead a team when you question plans or focus on potential failure. You must exhibit a strong will to minimize the chances of failure. However, if events are not going well, you may need to withdraw from the group temporarily, get time alone, and make adjustments to the plan to ensure success. Constant adjustment is crucial to getting to a desired outcome. It does no good to be stubborn about a plan that is not working.

Combat individual or group negativity immediately and crush it. It can spiral out of control if not quickly checked. If people are allowed to focus on all the things that could go wrong, they will. Negativity or sarcasm can become pervasive if not checked early and will compromise the team's effectiveness and its ability to execute the plan on time. Be sure to check yourself to see if you are communicating a negative or critical attitude.

Keep team members focused on the major initiatives that are to be fulfilled and continually relate them to the mission and goals of the organization. This will consistently reinforce why the initiatives are important to the bigger picture and should stem any lack of motivation. You have to major in the major issues, not major in minor issues. The greatest results come only when you have your team focused on the items that matter most to the organization. Too many leaders project a distracted focus that confuses those who are following them. An overabundance of initiatives will water down the key goals, which will become lost in the process. Strategic adjustments and constant reprioritization are necessary, but once the course is determined, stay focused on the directives that enable the major initiatives to be accomplished.

Openness

Be open to people and their ideas regardless of their job roles, organizational levels, or experience so you can gather all pertinent information before acting on a goal or plan. In addition, glean information from your network of people outside your team to draw on best practices before acting on a plan.

Promote an environment where people can give genuine input and feedback. Solicit people's most original and creative ideas and ask how they would apply them to targeted initiatives. Fortunately, most organizational cultures today dictate that open feedback and communication are essential to motivate people to perform a task and buy into a vision or plan. If you consistently ask people what they are thinking, you will gain insight into their engagement, motivation, and commitment.

You need to have a certain degree of transparency because showing some emotion will let people know that you care. This will help you develop trust more quickly. If you show that you have nothing to hide, you are modeling behavior that others will potentially follow. Honest and forthright communication breaks down walls and enables people to get on the same page and progress rapidly.

While nurturing and promoting an open environment is necessary, you also need to communicate that while all ideas and suggestions are important, the leadership is responsible for making any final decisions. Openness does not mean that you require subordinate approval to move forward. Leadership and hierarchical organizational structures are tasked with making decisions relative to the mission, vision, and goals of an organization. They have ultimate accountability for implementation of tactical plans and results.

As a leader, you are not always going to be right in your personal assessment of a situation. You may experience a sense of trepidation or question a plan or decision. However, there comes a time when all input has been reviewed and a decision has to be made and a plan enacted. At such a time, you must present the plan with boldness and will. Always remember to relate the plan back to the mission and goals of the organization. Expressing unequivocal conviction when rolling out a goal or plan will give others confidence and single-mindedness.

You need to have the openness, boldness, and courage to put your plan and yourself out there for evaluation and be prepared to deal with both the positive recognition and the criticism that may result.

Quick Reference

Your team is always watching and critiquing your behavior. Because team members will follow you only if they believe you are authentic, you need to develop personal strengths.

Setting the Example

- You are held to higher standards than the people you manage.
- You have to set an example for the behavior you want from your team because people learn more from observing your behavior than from what you say to them.
- When you admit your own mistakes, you create a safe environment for others to take risks.
- Pointing out people's mistakes, helping them learn from their mistakes, and keeping them motivated in the process is an art.

Self-Assessment

- You need to develop the ability to consistently, honestly, and objectively assess your strengths and weaknesses.
- Your greatest impact on others comes when you share your strength areas with team members.
- Great leaders are committed to being lifelong learners.

Awareness

- Leaders need to be aware of patterns and trends and anticipate situations before they occur.
- You can develop a consistent, long-term success pattern by staying on an even keel emotionally and remaining aware of the big picture.
- Good leaders are aware of individual motivational needs and address them promptly.

Emotional Strength

- Your emotional strength is vital to sustain your team's motivation. It will enable you to face a problem or challenge and devise a solution without getting overwhelmed.
- You need to keep challenges in perspective and stay calm in the face of adversity.
- Strong leaders view problems or negative circumstances as a way to develop character.
- When the heat is turned up, exceptional leaders are at their best.

Discipline

- Consistency in daily activities reinforces your leadership and projects discipline.
- Doing tasks you don't want to do without complaining is a form of self-discipline. Your team will notice.
- Preparation is a discipline that sets people apart in any endeavor.

Will and Focus

- You must set the tone by expressing without hesitation or doubt that an initiative will be realized.
- The greatest results come only when you have the team focused on the items that matter most to the organization.
- Too many initiatives will water down the key goals, which will become lost in the process.

Openness

- You need to keep asking people what they think and promote an environment where they give genuine input and feedback.
- You should be open and listen to others regardless of their position so you can gather all the pertinent information before you act on a plan.
- Openness is important, but ultimately the leadership is responsible for making final decisions.

Chapter 3

Implementing the Mission, Vision, and Culture

A N ORGANIZATION'S MISSION, vision, and culture need to be constantly reinforced and kept in the forefront of every organizational and departmental communication. Leaders must find practical ways to relate them to all goals, plans, and daily activities.

Mission

Every leader needs to understand the mission of the organization intimately and be able to apply it to all concrete initiatives. In times of challenge or doubt, you need the anchor of the mission to guide your decision making.

Keep the mission in the forefront so all members of the organization incorporate it into their daily duties. You need to communicate it repeatedly and consistently to keep the organization on track. When you regularly convey the significance of the mission, people will see how their work benefits the group as a whole.

For example, the Acme School District, one of the fictitious organizations in this book, has the following mission: "Develop lifelong learners who can pursue academic achievement in their individual learning styles and are connected to the community." This mission needs to be part of everything the district does, so, as you will see in chapter 4, it appears on the rolling agendas the district uses for weekly meetings. In this way the district leaders make sure that even the smallest task relates directly to the mission. In part 3 you will see how Acme also uses the mission statement in job descriptions and in the information base that members of the organization use when they talk to others about the district.

Your job is to establish the key goals of the organization and show how they relate to the mission. The mission and goals must be communicated to new members as well as those who have spent considerable time with the organization. Many leaders assume the mission will be understood and they don't need to speak in detail about why the organization exists and what it is called to do. However, both new and veteran people in the organization need to be reminded of it often or the organization can develop mission drift, which will make it vulnerable.

The mission of an organization can be adapted or changed based on current conditions, but the foundational mission premise should not be altered significantly. Keep the mission simple so people can accurately and readily articulate it as part of the organization's information base (more about this in chapter 8).

Vision

Visionary leadership is the responsibility of all leaders and managers at different levels in an organization. You must give your people a vision that is larger than they are. The ability to stay ahead of your team by anticipating needs and challenges is a must in leadership and will be discussed in more detail in part 2 of this book. You need to strike an effective balance between developing an ongoing vision and executing short-term initiatives. To do this means you must make time to get away from the tyranny of the urgent and chart the course of the team you manage. This entails assessment of long- and short-term needs and requires time to think, plan, adjust, and stay ahead of the group. If you are constantly in a reactive mode, the mission will suffer.

Communicate the vision of the big picture continually so that all goals and plans relate directly to the mission and all people remain on the same page. People are eager to be viewed as being significant and must feel that they are accomplishing tasks that help achieve a common cause. Your ability to communicate the vision will inspire others and galvanize their commitment to the common cause.

Organizations are either growing or dying; there is very little middle ground. To keep an organization growing, change and adjustment need to be an integral part of planning to advance any team. However, if the leader attempts to institute changes without a well-thought-out set of goals and plans, failure will occur. The desired changes can come about only when plans are implemented in a calculated manner and the changes relate to the vision of the organization.

Although you need to be able to see the big picture and to visualize events from differing perspectives, the vision will be fulfilled only when each individual owns it and can articulate it properly. People who cannot articulate the mission and vision probably don't understand them and don't see them as relevant to their work. The organization as a whole must be unified in a mission and vision or achieving the desired outcomes will be impossible. In an individualistic society like ours, it is common for people to have individual missions, visions, goals and agendas that hinder overall organizational achievement. Your job is to bring people together in a unified vision.

Let's use the example of the fictitious LGLO Specialty Shoe Store. Store owner Chris and store manager Karen were faced with a challenge: a new staff member, Chad, was too focused on his own agenda. A key goal for LGLO was customer satisfaction through teamwork. Chad was focused only on his own sales and was neglecting other customers in the store or trying to make sales to customers who were already engaged with other LGLO employees.

To bring people together into a unified vision, Karen had to address the situation: "Chad, I know you are new to LGLO and you're doing a good job. We need to discuss one issue. The vision of LGLO is to prioritize customer satisfaction and foster teamwork in a highly ethical environment. At times I have seen you neglect customers or try to sell to customers who are already engaged with other LGLO employees. Can you please be more aware of other customers and try to assist other members of the team in the future? I know that you may have come from other organizations with different visions and operating styles, but LGLO is very committed to our mission and vision. Do you think you can make this adjustment in how you work? Do you think this is the right place for you to work based on the vision of teamwork and customer satisfaction? Chris and I think you are doing well learning the job so far, and we want to continue to help you develop."

In this example, notice how Karen framed the area of needed improvement with two positive statements.

Culture

Organizational cultures take on the personalities of the executives and higher level managers. Most organizations can be broken down culturally into three primary categories: strategic, tactical, and reactive.

Strategic organizations are those that have definitive structures, communication, and planning. People know their roles and what is expected of them. Strategic organizations are characterized by stability, consistent growth, and low turnover.

Tactical organizations have structure but struggle to propagate their mission and goals over extended periods. Their culture is characterized by higher level management turnover and dependence on key individuals who cannot be easily replaced. They experience low to moderate growth that they find difficult to sustain.

Reactive organizations can only respond to what's urgent because they don't have systematic processes or structures to deal with challenges or opportunities. Their culture is characterized by high overall turnover, especially in management, and lack of executive breadth and depth. Reactive organizations experience growth swings but will ultimately fail because they cannot overcome their organizational and leadership dysfunction.

To understand strategic, tactical, and reactive cultures, let's see what LGLO Specialty Shoe Store would be like with each type of organizational culture.

The strategic LGLO has stable ownership and has grown at 20 percent per year over the last five years. It has had the same four employees and has invested in them from both financial and personal development standpoints. The strategic LGLO's mission, goals, and plans are being accomplished through good management without major changes. Although slight adjustments are consistently made to help better achieve goals, the organization does not suffer from mission drift or an identity crisis. The strategic LGLO is active in the community and is constantly in touch with best practices that could be implemented to help it further improve. The strategic LGLO is characterized by good customer and employee satisfaction.

With a tactical culture, LGLO has stable ownership and is growing at 10 percent per year. It has had the same owner and manager the last five years but experiences an average eighteen-month turnover in staff positions. The organization has trouble replacing staff, which puts stress on management. The manager hires less-experienced staff who may or may not be the right fit for the organization because she doesn't have time to recruit more candidates. LGLO's mission and goals have stayed the same, but its plans are constantly changing because the organization is falling short of its goals. If the manager at the tactical LGLO were to leave, the organization would be in serious trouble because she is holding the place together. The organization is characterized by acceptable customer satisfaction but poor employee satisfaction, as evidenced by turnover.

The reactive LGLO has had the same owner and is experiencing zero to negative growth annually. It averages a twelve- to eighteen-month turnover at the store manager position. The owner has to work in the store and does not see investing in the store manager as a good strategy because it costs too much money. The store staff average turnover is twelve months, and the owner is just trying to keep the doors open. He frequently changes the mission and goals of the reactive LGLO so he can take advantage of short-term opportunities. This leads to a lack of continuity, and the owner is trying to determine how he can sell the store. The reactive LGLO has poor customer and employee satisfaction.

Culture is critical to all teams as it ultimately reflects individual motivations to carry out the mission and goals. Without a common culture, organizations tend to fragment into subcultures with differing views on how to achieve the overall mission. Setting and nurturing the culture is the primary role of executive management. A strong, positive organizational culture will promote and sustain the organization's mission and vision.

The word "culture" comes from "cultivate," which suggests that a culture needs to be constantly worked at and reinforced. Culture is not only the intangible feel of an organization but also its sense of purpose and drive. Positive cultures create organizational momentum and allow for great things to be accomplished. Peer motivation is established, and higher expectations and accountabilities can then be realized.

Leaders must always monitor the culture in their organization. One way you can have a positive impact on your organizational culture is to constantly assess customer satisfaction and employee satisfaction. Customer satisfaction tells you how well you are doing outside the organization, and employee satisfaction measures internal organizational wellness.

However, you can't measure employee satisfaction from atop the organization. You have to frequently touch all levels of your organization to take a real temperature of the culture. A good practice is to converse with both longtime, trusted members of the organization and new people. This will give you insight into the entire spectrum of the organization.

If you think your organization is operating strategically, continue to nurture your best practices. Don't ever think the culture doesn't need constant care and cultivation. It does. To avoid stagnation, apply best practices from other organizations.

In many organizations, different departments can have different cultures. As a leader you must make sure to bring these departments together, unify their cultures, and lead the people toward the organization's mission, vision, and goals. If you see parts of the organization in tactical or reactive mode, quickly try to get them back to operating in a strategic mode.

To move from a tactical to a strategic culture, make sure to go through a checklist of basics. For example, is the proper structure in place to propagate your mission and goals over an extended period of time? Are your managers and key employees happy and buying into the organization's culture? Focus on these areas. As leaders move into higher positions in an organization, they have less contact with their customers and constituents. It is paramount that you focus your attention on your key managers and employees because they are touching your constituency and are an extension of you.

Moving from a reactive to a strategic culture is much more difficult and may require some foundational changes. Reactive organizations typically can only respond to what's urgent and have a hard time dealing with challenges. They may experience a few successes here and there, but that doesn't mean these organizations are healthy. Leadership is the key factor in moving to a strategic culture. If you are in a reactive culture, get back to the basics of your mission with a few key leaders and determine how you can move forward. Revisit the foundations of who you are and what you do. Reactive organizations are often characterized by having a single leader trying to do everything. A reactive organization cannot move forward with a single leader.

Reactive cultures need simplification and structure. As a leader, focus on your mission and a few key goals. Be realistic about what goals you can achieve and then formulate well-thought-out strategic plans that can be executed to accomplish the goals. Try not to add too many initiatives or you will find yourself back in a reactive mode. You have to reestablish the organization's foundation and surround yourself with people who can help you move forward. For more specific help on upgrading your culture, see "Adjusting Plans for Greater Effectiveness" in chapter 5.

Quick Reference

An organization's mission, vision, and culture are crucial to its success. Part of your job as a leader is to understand these elements of your organization and find ways to implement them in practical forms so your team can see that they are a part of every daily task.

Mission

- You need to understand the mission of the organization intimately and be able to apply it to all initiatives and decisions.
- You must remind both new and veteran people in the organization of the mission. Unless everyone is focused on the mission, mission drift can occur.

Vision

- People need to be given a vision that is larger than they are.
- You must try to strike an effective balance between an ongoing vision and short-term initiatives.
- People are eager to feel that they are accomplishing tasks that help achieve a common cause.

- Team members who cannot articulate the mission and vision probably don't understand them or see them as relevant to their work.

Culture

- Organizational cultures take on the personalities of the executives and higher level managers.
- Most organizations fall into three cultural categories: strategic, tactical, and reactive.
- Without a common culture, organizations tend to fragment into subcultures with differing views and no common idea about achieving the overall mission.
- Leaders need to constantly monitor and cultivate the culture of their organization.

Management

M ANAGEMENT IS THE ability to handle or direct people skill-fully and to succeed in accomplishing goals. Managers need strong leadership skills that they use effectively to achieve results. This part of the book will more closely examine the necessities and qualities of leadership and directly apply them to management principles.

The primary task in all management positions is to execute the mission, vision, goals, and plans of an organization, so managers need to fully understand all organizational priorities. This understanding facilitates an environment where they can set appropriate goals, develop applicable plans, and ultimately execute those plans. When managers are intimately familiar with the organization's priorities, they can more easily inspire others to buy into, share in, and take part in the organization's mission and goals. The best plans are developed and enacted based on an individual manager's strengths, experiences, and resources. Good managers must be able to adjust quickly to keep plans directed toward executing the intended objectives.

The ability to execute initiatives will set you apart as a manager. The circumstances, complexity, and demands of a project can become overwhelming, but by simplifying a project into manageable tasks, you can reduce the number of variables and organize a plan more easily. Once a plan is organized properly, it is much easier to execute and manage throughout its life cycle.

Managers have a variety of roles, including leader, coach, counselor, listener, motivator, organizer, and initiator. At all times good managers must have the leadership skills to motivate team members and partner with them for success. As with leadership, you develop management skills every day by building on the skills you have already learned and applying them to new circumstances.

Part 2 offers tactical management skills, techniques for team development, and interpersonal management skills that will help you execute your organization's mission and vision.

CHAPTER 4

Executing Your Organization's Mission and Vision

A S MENTIONED IN part 1, having an in-depth knowledge of the organization's mission and vision is critical to a manager. The mission is the anchor of any organization. It is the foundation upon which all goals, initiatives, and team cohesion should be built. To retain the proper long-term focus, people must feel included and useful in the accomplishment of the mission. This chapter offers tools to accomplish that goal. It also addresses how to

- Develop goals relative to the organizational mission
- Plan to achieve those goals
- Devise executable tasks and actions to fulfill the plans

You will also learn about a tool called the "rolling agenda," which will help you put plans, tasks, and actions into a tangible format so you can execute and manage them in a way that leads toward accomplishing your organization's mission.

Setting Goals Based on the Mission and Vision

The objective of goal setting is to operationalize the mission and vision of an organization. Goal setting should enable team members to see how their work contributes toward the larger objective. This personalizes the mission and helps them relate to the organization with a sense of pride and ownership. You should define all goals in the context of the mission and high-level organizational initiatives. Break larger goals down into achievable plans, tasks, and actions such that the tasks have specific relevance to the mission. Each task ought to have clearly defined roles and time frames associated with it. To see how this works in practice, let's look at a fictitious company, the Bright Future Tutoring franchise.

The Bright Future Tutoring franchise had a very clear mission: assist children to build routines that will help them succeed both inside and outside the classroom. Jim, the manager of one center, could not understand why his center lacked a motivated workforce and a steady clientele. The center a few miles away, managed by Judy, hired students from the same university and drew clients from the same neighborhood that Jim did. Judy's team was a vibrant group with a low turnover rate. The team members had developed relationships with the center's students and produced results that pleased the parents.

Jim, on the other hand, had a very high turnover rate of employees who were clock watchers, counting down the minutes until they could leave. His team members often spent time socializing with each other or studying for their college courses. They appeased difficult children with games rather than encouraging them to engage in the franchise's study activities. It didn't matter whether Jim tried to threaten them or bribe them; the employees were simply not yielding positive results.

Jim complained to Judy that although their hiring procedures, wages, and job expectations for employees were identical, his tutors seemed much less motivated. Judy explained her technique of holding monthly "target talks." Parents were entitled to a monthly meeting with their child, Judy, and one or two tutors. During these meetings they would discuss realistic objectives for the student, such as getting an improved grade on a math test, reading a book without help, and so on. When the child met an objective, the parent was able to recognize a tangible accomplishment and Judy was able to commend her team member for a job well done. The team enjoyed a personal sense of accomplishment, and Judy consistently made them aware of their success and their value in the overall mission. Jim could see how his own team had a very vague understanding of how to accomplish the mission of Bright Future Tutoring, so he replicated Judy's target talks in his center to give his employees tangible goals and a sense of ownership within the organization.

Like Judy, managers must see the mission in the details of their work and create specific goals that align with that mission. Good managers can visualize the mission being accomplished in advance. They develop tangible goals, plans that help people meet those goals, and executable tasks that fulfill the plans. Through foresight and clear planning, managers chip away everything that will not lead to the achievement of the goals. As a result, team members can see clearly where they fit in the organization and how their work contributes to the mission.

Part of the goal-setting process should include granting autonomy and authority for team members to carry out the mission in their individual tasks. If executives and managers constantly micromanage the achievement of goals, team members will never own the mission themselves. Managers must learn to delegate work to team members so that the organization can grow and scale efficiently. Delegation, one of the most difficult tactical management skills to learn, will be examined in chapter 5.

As mentioned in chapter 1, the most critical resource in any organization is its people. You have a unique opportunity to develop and mentor people through goal setting and delegation. Judy took the time to recognize and celebrate when key tasks or goals were achieved. You too should always be intentional about demonstrating appreciation for such accomplishments because they directly relate to advancing the organizational mission. Appreciation reinforces the behaviors that lead to the accomplishment of goals and it sustains motivation.

In our fast-paced society it's easy to move forward too quickly without giving proper recognition or demonstrating appreciation of an accomplishment. As a manager, you need to develop the habit of saying "Thank you for the effort" and "Good job" frequently. Be sure to express genuine appreciation. If you don't, these phrases can appear contrived or patronizing and will be dismissed quickly. Thankfulness is a key part of leadership and management. It communicates to your team members that you have stopped and taken the time to recognize their effort. Thankfulness positively influences the health, outlook, and vitality of both the giver and the recipient.

Don't forget to recognize the efforts and goal fulfillment of those who are relatively new to the organization. These people have yet to cultivate their identities in the team. Establishing a positive base will likely result in a positive working relationship. Although positive recognition is often reserved for team members with longer organizational tenure, including new people in the recognition process is a good practice.

Planning to Achieve Goals

Strategically devised plans and their subsequent execution determine your success in reaching the goals you set. If you fail to plan, you plan to fail. Too many managers rush into activities without proper planning, and the results are poor or mediocre at best. Excellent results, not busyness or activity, are the objective. Good managers allocate the requisite time to assess all the variables and then integrate their conclusions into well-thought-out plans that can help people meet their organizational goals. Assessing risk and the amount of organizational change associated with a plan before it is enacted is critical so you can determine how quickly the plan will become effective. Plans must be painstakingly specific to achieve the desired goals and in turn contribute to the fulfillment of the mission.

"Strategic Thinking" in chapter 1 offers several concepts that apply when formulating effective plans. One of the concepts is to always keep track of the big picture and communicate it emphatically to the people you manage when you present a plan. Another suggestion is to be in a continual state of evaluation and adjustment because plans very rarely work well the first time.

Strategically adjusting a plan without getting caught up in overanalysis is a delicate balancing act. Too much dissection can cause unnecessary delays in the achievement of goals. Thoroughly consider the variables and enact the first complete iteration of the plan with focus and will. This will advance the momentum necessary for achieving the desired goals. You can then make adjustments and course corrections as you move closer to the goals so you achieve the preferred results.

The framework and methodology for planning are also important. An annual plan related to the organization's mission and goals is critical as a road map. However, quarterly and even monthly adjustments are necessary to get the annual plan more closely aligned to the stated goals and to prevent it from collecting dust.

An annual plan (and subsequent adjustments) ought to be prepared by each individual team member. Each team member should link his or her plan to the organizational priorities for the year. These priorities should relate directly to the mission. Individual planning within an organizational context will enable each team member to feel empowered to make decisions and take risks within his or her area of responsibility.

Goals and plans have to be clearly defined, accurate, and realistic. Additionally, planning ought to reflect departmental goals. When you set goals on an organizational, departmental, and individual level, those goals should provide a cohesive framework for action. Always consider organizational and individual strengths as you plan for key goals to be accomplished.

Be sure to list the organization's mission and goals at the top of any plan, task list, or agenda. This technique provides team members with an easy reference and reinforces the relevance of the goals and mission to their daily activities and responsibilities.

Developing Tasks to Execute Plans

Execution is the key element in management success and the true measure of effectiveness. Without strategic execution, the best plans are useless.

The ability to execute a plan is based on categorizing the key elements into achievable tasks, often referred to as the "task approach." The task approach enables team members to focus on achieving specific objectives without feeling overwhelmed by the size of a project. You need to assign and guide the execution of tasks while allowing team members the autonomy to accomplish them as they see best. You can enhance this process by consistently communicating the organization's mission and stressing the relevance of task completion to the mission's fulfillment.

When planning, carefully consider the material and human resources available to execute an objective properly. Assign tasks to individuals who have previously shown the ability to accomplish them or to those who have clearly demonstrated the aptitude for increased responsibility. Never assign tasks that exceed an individual's skill set or experience because doing so could compromise the execution of a plan. Remember that lessons learned through past successes and failures form people's educational foundation and are a good predictor of their future success. You need to be strategic and deliberate when assigning tasks and should think through the positive and negative implications of your decisions.

Involving individuals in the assignment of tasks is critical to the successful execution of plans and achievement of goals. Individual buy-in lays the foundation for the accomplishment of key goals. Collective and individual ownership of the stated goals will help establish momentum toward fulfilling the organization's mission.

You must balance team members' input with your own vision of how a plan should be executed. Most people are fairly objective when they assess their own capabilities so factor in their assessments before assigning tasks. People's development is important, but assigning tasks that exceed their current skill and experience levels is in neither the individual's nor the team's best interest.

Most of the collaborative input is needed in the initial stages of plan development. As you finalize the execution plan, you'll need less input from team members.

The mission and goals are typically determined at the executive levels of any organization. Planning for how they are accomplished is most often formulated at the departmental level, and this is where consensus-building input is most necessary. Remember that you must consistently assess and address individual team members' motivation to ensure a goal, plan, or task is completed effectively.

Completing Tasks

Once tasks are assigned, you must inspect and measure them until they are completed. This requires that you be consistent but not overbearing.

An action is something that must be done to accomplish a task. Descriptions of actions need to be specific, and metrics must be assigned so that team members clearly understand what is required. The descriptions should revolve around the nature of the task, how the task is to be accomplished, when it should be done, and who will do it.

Good communication is always important, but it is even more critical in this part of the process. If communication is lacking, tasks are either not achieved or they take excessive time to be executed. When managing task and action completion, use the ideas from the "Communication" section in chapter 1. Remember that communication needs to be clear, frequent, and easily understood. Use confirmations and directed questions to ensure team members clearly understand your expectations. State repeatedly and specifically when tasks need to be completed. This kind of effective communication will result in the accomplishment of actions.

For an example of directed questions, let's look at a key Customer Satisfaction goal at LGLO Specialty Shoe Stores. Manager Karen has delegated the task of auditing the amount of referral and repeat business to her assistant manager, Joe. He is to assess the percentage of monthly sales that are repeat or referral based and provide a written report on the fifth of each month.

Karen will communicate with Joe weekly about the task. Making sure her communication is clear, frequent, and easily understood, Karen will ask him each Friday how the repeat and referral sales are tracking for the week and for the month. By doing this, Karen will reinforce the high priority of the task and make sure LGLO is meeting its customer satisfaction goal. The weekly directed questions could be, "Joe, how are we doing this week on repeat and referral sales? We were a little shy of our goal last week. What can we do to make sure we stay on track for the month?"

Many organizations dawdle in the execution of key goals and initiatives because their managers do not effectively manage daily, weekly, and monthly tasks. If you don't create a sense of urgency about tasks, they will roll from week to week, month to month, and potentially year to year. This delay can be fatal to an organization. You must insist that all actions be executed on time. This case study of the imaginary Fox Designs company shows why.

Fox Designs was a small clothing company run by the Fox family. Jacob Fox was the acting CEO, and other family members were placed in vital management positions. The company rapidly expanded, and soon it was clear that Fox Designs should aim to manufacture and distribute its products internationally.

A variety of tasks needed to be done to accomplish this goal, and Jacob delegated these tasks in a fragmented manner. One person was in charge of establishing a factory in China, another person was in charge of dealing with Chinese regulations on the company's products, and yet another person was in charge of shipping the products internationally.

The Fox Designs office soon became an extremely tense environment. Members of the Fox family felt that for every one task accomplished, at least ten more would spring up. With a great deal of juggling, Fox Designs was successful in cost-effectively manufacturing its products in China and shipping to seven countries. Then Jacob received a call from US Customs.

As it turned out, Fox Designs had neglected to pay a variety of fees associated with overseas manufacturing and shipping. Jacob was stunned to find out that his company owed hundreds of thousands of dollars in duty, money that had not been calculated in the company's costs. He was furious with the team members, believing that one of them had been negligent. Ultimately, Jacob was the one who had been negligent: he had not properly coordinated the necessary tasks and he hadn't followed up to make sure everything was on track toward the goal of making Fox Designs an international company.

Action execution leads to task completion, which leads to the execution of plans and the fulfillment of goals. Jacob, however, had created a disjointed environment where it was difficult for all the necessary tasks to be completed. As we saw in chapter 1, creating an environment where tasks can be completed will create momentum. You can use task completion to instill confidence and reinforce the momentum necessary to achieve greater things.

The team members at Fox Designs felt defeated in their jobs; they never experienced satisfaction after completing a task because there was always more to do and they never had a chance to catch their breath. As a manager, Jacob failed to recognize the lack of cohesion and organization that burdened his team until the drastic costs of his negligence became apparent.

When tasks are completed successfully and people's hard work is recognized, team members gain more confidence in the plan and negative thoughts or feelings dissipate. Remember that momentum on a plan is created when members are contributing and attaining good results simultaneously and sequentially.

The Fox family became demoralized when they were only intermittently able to carry out tasks for a seemingly unattainable plan. On the other hand, if team members had focused on completing their individual actions and tasks, then the plan might have seemed within reach. People would have seen the fruits of their labor, so they would have gained confidence and been motivated to take on bigger and more difficult challenges in the future. However, Fox Designs loaded its team with a never-ending list of tasks. The team members' lack of success on this plan might cause them to shy away from future challenges associated with growth. In the future, Jacob may decide to improve his system so that team members can enjoy the satisfaction of completed tasks. If he does, the team will gain self-assurance and an enthusiasm for future goals.

Using Rolling Agendas

One helpful tool for completing tasks is the rolling agenda, a one- to two- page document that organizes and simplifies the execution process. It provides a way to sequentially execute an organization's mission, goals, plans, actions, and tasks. Two rolling agendas are provided here as examples to illustrate the execution process. The two organizations are fictitious, and the content of these examples is of secondary importance. What's essential is understanding the Rolling Agenda's concepts, process, and flow and how it enables managerial execution. These two examples show how the Rolling Agenda can be applied in a wide spectrum of fields and disciplines.

LGLO Specialty Shoe Store

The first example is for LGLO Specialty Shoe Store, whose mission is to help people in a profitable manner. Management sets goals based on the organization's values and has developed a plan that addresses fulfillment of those goals. The Rolling Agenda includes a set of tasks and actions that will enable the organization to meet its plan, achieve its goals, and fulfill its mission. As you study the document, you will see how each task and action is related to the plan, goals, and mission of the organization.

The "Tasks (Action Details)" section is the key element and the benchmark for execution. If the tasks are not executed properly, the plan will not be successful and ultimately the goals and mission will not be achieved. Actions are what must be done to accomplish the task.

Each task is assigned to someone who is responsible for completing that task. If a deadline exists, that is included too. The assigned staff member and the time frame are included in the "action details." They are noted in parentheses next to the task for easy tracking and written in bold to stand out.

Having a Rolling Agenda like these will enable you to consistently keep your organization's mission and goals in the forefront of all communication to your team members. By using the Rolling Agenda for weekly meetings, you can measure progress, highlight accomplishments, create urgency in areas that are falling behind, and make adjustments to the tasks and plans when necessary.

Be sure to prepare an agenda for every meeting regardless of the meeting's importance. No agenda means no meeting. This practice will enable you to be more organized as well as transfer this discipline to your subordinates.

Rolling Agenda: LGLO Specialty Shoe Store

January 2 Weekly Rolling Agenda

Mission: The mission of LGLO is to help people physically, educationally, and socially as a profitable company.

GOALS

1. Create customer satisfaction, which is the key to success.
2. Create a store environment that rewards entrepreneurship, daily employee motivation, and teamwork in a highly ethical environment.

3. Motivate employees by providing an opportunity to gain wealth and advance their personal development.

4. Take calculated risks when necessary to fulfill the mission and goals.

5. Become a part of the local community and contribute 10% of annual profits to a local charity.

PLAN

Goal 1: Because customer satisfaction is a priority, LGLO will measure it by verbally asking in-store customers about their experience, mailing a five-question customer satisfaction survey, and tracking repeat business and referrals. Customer satisfaction will also be addressed by providing a socially friendly store environment.

Goal 2: The store environment will be measured subjectively and objectively. Subjective evaluation will be assessed based on employee self-motivation to go above and beyond expectations and observation of teamwork with other employees. Daily performance will be evaluated based on special-offer sales execution.

Goal 3: Wealth and advancement goals will be addressed by offering employees training opportunities for certifications and the ability to build an equity stake in LGLO with exceptional annual performance.

Goal 4: Risk goals will be targeted in the form of new doctor referral and diabetic Medicare programs.

Goal 5: Local community involvement will encompass regular attendance at service organization meetings and investigation of local charities for LGLO profit contributions.

TASKS (ACTION DETAILS)

Goal 1: Customer Satisfaction

- Ask every customer who enters the store an open-ended question about his or her experience. (**Action involves all staff and task is ongoing.**)
- Mail five-question customer satisfaction survey the first of each month to all customers who visited the store in

that month. Follow up by phone within two weeks of mailer. (**Manager Karen to mail on January 2 and to accomplish calls by January 15.**)

- Audit amount of referral and repeat business. (**Joe to assess monthly the percentage of sales that are repeat or referral based. Assessment is due the 5th of each month.**)

- Maintain positive store environment through cleanliness, furniture placement to promote conversations, and refreshments to enable a friendly environment. (**Chad, daily action.**)

Goal 2: Entrepreneurship, Motivation, Teamwork

- Store manager to assess employee motivation, self-direction, ability to handle multiple customers simultaneously, and teamwork. (**Manager Karen, daily.**)

- Owner to measure store manager and staff sales execution of daily specials. (**Owner Chris to measure monthly sales of specials and report to ownership group on the 15th of each month.**)

Goal 3: Compensation

- Certified pedorthist exam passed for $1,000 bonus. (**Joe, Chad to accomplish by June 15.**)

- One percent equity stake annually earned by exceeding sales targets. (**Karen, Joe, Chad to be reviewed by ownership group on December 31.**)

Goal 4: Risk

- Visit top 10 diabetic Medicare doctors who reside within a five-mile radius of the store. (**Karen to accomplish by January 30.**)

- Visit next 40 diabetic Medicare doctors. (**Joe to accomplish by February 15.**)

- Promote diabetic Medicare program to store customers. (**All staff, ongoing.**)

- Send diabetic Medicare mailer to 500-person list. **(Chad, by February 28.)**
- Visit top 50 local doctors to introduce referral program. **(Karen, Joe to accomplish by March 1.)**
- Mailer to 150 local doctors to introduce referral program **(Chad to accomplish by February 15.)**

Goal 5: Community Involvement/Contributions
- Research local service organizations including Rotary, Lions, and Kiwanis. **(Karen, by January 31.)**
- Interview local nonprofits, shelters, and so on for potential charitable contributions. **(Owner Chris, by March 15.)**

Updated Rolling Agenda

An updated rolling agenda is provided to illustrate how the weekly tasks and actions can change. In this example, the revised agenda shows the tactical adjustments that have been made over a six-week period. The mission and goals have stayed the same, which is typical of most organizations. The plan is also intact because the goals are being accomplished within the specified time periods.

Adjustments have been made in the "Task (Action Details)" portion of the agenda. Under goal 1, the task of mailing customer surveys was modified because the majority of surveys were not returned. It was decided to include a $20 discount coupon that could be used by the customer if the survey was returned. The tasks and action details for goals 2 and 3 remain the same.

The goal 4 tasks have had several changes. It was determined that it was productive to visit only the top ten diabetic Medicare doctors, so the task of visiting the additional forty doctors was deleted. Additionally the diabetic Medicare mailer was scrapped because it did not produce positive results. Likewise, in the referral program, it was deemed that the doctor visits were productive but that the mailer was not, so this task was deleted. During the course of the doctor visits, it was determined that physical therapists were also a great referral source, so that task was added to the list for goal 4.

Finally, goal 5 was adjusted to reflect the progress that was made.

The Rolling Agenda is an excellent tool to keep activities organized and establish a simple framework to execute objectives. It also brings momentum and rhythm to daily task achievement.

Updated Rolling Agenda: LGLO Specialty Shoe Store

February 15 Weekly Rolling Agenda

Mission: The mission of LGLO is to help people physically, educationally, and socially as a profitable company.

GOALS

1. Create customer satisfaction, which is the key to success.
2. Create a store environment that rewards entrepreneurship, daily employee motivation, and teamwork in a highly ethical environment.
3. Motivate employees by providing an opportunity to gain wealth and advance their personal development.
4. Take calculated risks when necessary to fulfill the mission and goals.
5. Become a part of the local community and contribute 10% of annual profits to a local charity.

PLAN

Goal 1: Because customer satisfaction is a priority, LGLO will measure it by verbally asking in-store customers about their experience, mailing a five-question customer satisfaction survey, and tracking repeat business and referrals. Customer satisfaction will also be addressed by providing a socially friendly store environment.

Goal 2: The store environment will be measured subjectively and objectively. Subjective evaluation will be assessed based on employee self-motivation to go above and beyond expectations and observation of teamwork with other employees. Daily performance will be evaluated based on daily special-offer sales execution.

Goal 3: Wealth and advancement goals will be addressed by offering employees training opportunities for certifications and the ability to build an equity stake in LGLO with exceptional annual performance.

Goal 4: Risk goals will be targeted in the form of new doctor referral and diabetic Medicare programs.

Goal 5: Local community involvement will encompass regular attendance at service organization meetings and investigation of local charities for LGLO profit contributions.

TASKS (ACTION DETAILS)

Goal 1: Customer Satisfaction

- Ask every customer who enters the store an open-ended question about his or her experience. **(Action involves all staff and task is ongoing.)**

- Mail five-question customer satisfaction survey the first of each month to all customers who visited the store that month. Follow up by phone within two weeks of mailer. Mail $20 discount coupon with survey to increase return rate. **(Karen to mail on February 15 with coupon and determine if it makes a difference. If surveys still are not returned, delete the task in the future. Make calls by March 1.)**

- Audit amount of referral and repeat business. **(Joe to assess monthly the percentage of sales that are repeat or referral based. Assessment is due the 5th of each month.)**

- Maintain positive store environment through cleanliness, furniture placement to promote conversations, and refreshments to enable a friendly environment. **(Chad, daily action.)**

Goal 2: Entrepreneurship, Motivation, Teamwork

- Store manager to assess employee motivation, self-direction, ability to handle multiple customers simultaneously, and teamwork. **(Manager Karen, daily.)**

- Owner to measure store manager and staff sales execution of daily specials. **(Owner Chris to measure monthly sales of specials and report to ownership group the 15th of each month.)**

Goal 3: Compensation

- Certified pedorthist exam passed for $1,000 bonus. **(Joe, Chad to accomplish by June 15.)**
- One percent equity stake annually earned by exceeding sales targets. **(Karen, Joe, Chad to be reviewed by ownership group on December 31.)**

Goal 4: Risk

- Visit top 10 diabetic Medicare doctors who reside within a five-mile radius of the store. **(Karen to accomplish by March 15.)**
- Promote diabetic Medicare program to store customers. **(All staff, ongoing.)**
- Visit top 50 local doctors to introduce referral program. **(Karen, Joe to accomplish by May 1.)**
- Visit top 25 physical therapists. **(Karen, Joe by May 1.)**

Goal 5: Community Involvement/Contributions

- Attend monthly Rotary and Kiwanis meetings. **(Karen through September 15; then reassess.)**
- Contribute 10% of annual profits to YMCA this year. **(Ownership team action by December 31.)**

Abbreviated Weekly Rolling Agenda

The full Rolling Agenda is great to use once a month to reinforce vital organizational initiatives. The next example is an abbreviated version that focuses strictly on the tasks and actions to be executed. This version is best used as a quick reference document for a weekly meeting. You can change any of the tasks or actions during the meeting to reflect progress, feedback, suggestions, and status updates. The abbreviated version affords you the ability to move quickly through the items.

Abbreviated Weekly Rolling Agenda: LGLO Specialty Shoe Store

January 10 Weekly Rolling Agenda

TASKS (ACTION DETAILS)

1. Weekly customer experience audit (round table, all staff)
2. Customer satisfaction survey mailer (Karen report)
3. Weekly referral/repeat business metrics (Joe report)
4. Store environment improvements (Chad; round table, all staff)
5. Staff teamwork improvements (Karen)
6. Daily special-sales execution (Chris)
7. Pedorthist certification progress (Karen)
8. Diabetic Medicare doctor visits (Karen, Joe)
9. In-store diabetic Medicare promotion (round table, all staff)
10. Diabetic Medicare mailer (Chad)
11. Doctor referral program visits (Karen, Joe)
12. Referral program mailer (Chad)
13. Local service organization development (Karen)

Acme School District

The organization in our second example, the Acme School District, has a mission to develop lifelong learners who are connected to the community. Goals and plans are developed to achieve the mission, and the Rolling Agenda keeps them in the forefront of daily tasks and actions.

Rolling Agenda: Acme School District

September 1 Weekly Rolling Agenda

Mission: Develop lifelong learners who can pursue academic achievement in their individual learning styles and are connected to the community.

GOALS

1. Create an environment in which students are motivated, achieve success, and enjoy learning.
2. Provide an academic support system that enables students to succeed to the best of their abilities.
3. Utilize a variety of methodologies to teach content in innovative ways to maximize student learning.
4. Give students an opportunity to become part of the community through a variety of experiences.

PLAN

Goal 1: The Acme School District will provide a host of opportunities for students to explore areas of interest and pursue them. The district will assess all students' current language and math levels and develop programs for students' individual advancement. Finding and developing interest areas and experiencing the success of advancement will result in student motivation and enjoyment of learning.

Goal 2: The Acme School District believes that the responsibility for the overall education of a child belongs to parents, teachers, educational administrators, and the community at large. Support will come through utilization of community service volunteers and secondary school volunteers to tutor in both the classroom environment and after-school programs. The focus will be on individualized student advancement.

Goal 3: Students have different learning styles, so a multimodal approach will be used. Instruction will be given in auditory, visual, and kinesthetic modes to make sure all students are being taught in their best learning style. State-standard-based content will be presented in a variety of ways with a heavy technology emphasis. Assessment will take place after each unit to make sure each student has mastered the state-standard-based content.

Goal 4: Students will have the opportunity to visit local assisted-living facilities, businesses, and museums to gain an appreciation and awareness of their community. Visits will take place during regular instruction hours as well as through supervised after-school trips. Parents and community volunteers will facilitate the visits.

TASKS (ACTION DETAILS)

Goal 1: Student Motivation, Success, and Enjoyment

- Teachers to show career awareness video. (**All teachers by September 15.**)

- Teachers to administer interests/skills assessments. (**Lead teacher at each school site by November 1.**)

- Teachers/aides/volunteers to match interest/skill test results for each student with career awareness choices to show education relevance. (**To be facilitated by classroom teachers for each student by December 1.**)

- District language and math assessments to be administered for each student. (**Each teacher to complete by October 15.**)

Goal 2: Academic Support

- District to develop screening and training program for volunteer classroom tutors. (**District training coordinator to complete by October 15.**)

- Secondary school students to be used as classroom tutors. (**Individual teachers to utilize tutors from 1:00 to 2:00 p.m. on Mondays, Wednesdays, and Thursdays.**)

- Community volunteers to be used in after-school tutoring program. (**Individual teachers to coordinate from 3:00 to 4:00 p.m. on Mondays, Wednesdays, and Thursdays.**)

- Individual assessment to be conducted to gauge math and language skill mastery. (**Individual teachers to conduct**

weekly until skill is mastered. When skill is mastered, teachers to move students to next skill and level per state standards.)

Goal 3: Learning Styles, Multimodal Instruction

- Learning style test to be administered to determine how each student best learns. **(Each teacher by October 15.)**
- State standards to be used as a baseline and comprise 90% of instruction. **(Site principal to inspect individual teacher lesson plans weekly to ensure compliance.)**
- Content to be taught in auditory, visual, and kinesthetic modes. **(Principal to inspect lesson plans weekly. Vice principal to observe individual teachers monthly.)**
- Computer lab programs to be used to reinforce content with individual students. **(Each teacher on Tuesdays and Thursdays at computer lab.)**
- Monthly tests to be administered to determine individual student content acquisition and establish new foundation. **(Each teacher to test by 15th of each month; adjust content and repeat monthly.)**

Goal 4: Community Connection

- Visits to local assisted-living facilities, businesses. and museums to be scheduled. **(Site PTA president by September 30.)**
- Community visits. **(PTA/community volunteers monthly during school hours.)**
- Students to apply learning from community visits. **(Each teacher to assign writing assignment following a visit. Assignment to be based on state standards and to be accomplished within two days of the visit.)**

Updated Rolling Agenda

The updated Rolling Agenda illustrates how the plan, weekly tasks, and actions can change. In this example, the revised agenda shows the tactical adjustments made over a six-week period. The mission and goals have stayed the same, which is typical of most organizations. The plan has been adjusted because some of the initial concepts did not work out. As the plan changed, the "Tasks (Action Details)" section was changed appropriately.

In the plan, goal 1 stays the same. Under goal 2, an adjustment has been made because the secondary school students were deemed not to be reliable tutors. Their involvement has been dropped from the plan and the accompanying task has been deleted. Goal 3 has stayed the same. Goal 4 has been adjusted because it was determined that the community visits during school hours took away from valuable core instruction time. The plan was amended so that the visits took place only after school hours. The task and action details were adjusted as well.

Updated Rolling Agenda: Acme School District

October 15 Revised Weekly Rolling Agenda

Mission: Develop lifelong learners who can pursue academic achievement in their individual learning styles and are connected to the community.

GOALS

1. Create an environment in which students are motivated, achieve success, and enjoy learning.

2. Provide an academic support system that enables students to succeed to the best of their abilities.

3. Utilize a variety of methodologies to teach content in innovative ways to maximize student learning.

4. Give students an opportunity to become part of the community through a variety of experiences.

PLAN

Goal 1: The Acme School District will provide a host of opportunities for students to explore areas of interest and pursue them. The district will assess all students' current language and math levels and develop programs for students' individual advancement. Finding and developing interest areas and experiencing the success of advancement will result in student motivation and enjoyment of learning.

Goal 2: The Acme School District believes that the responsibility for the overall education of a child belongs to parents, teachers, educational administrators, and the community at large. Support will come through utilization of community service volunteers to tutor in both the classroom environment and after-school tutoring programs. The focus will be on individualized student advancement.

Goal 3: Students have different learning styles, so a multimodal approach will be used. Instruction will be given in auditory, visual, and kinesthetic modes to make sure all students are being taught in their best learning style. State-standard-based content will be presented in a variety of ways with a heavy technology emphasis. Assessment will take place after each unit to make sure each student has mastered the state-standard-based content.

Goal 4: Students will have the opportunity to visit local assisted-living facilities, businesses, and museums to gain an appreciation and awareness of their community. Visits will take place through supervised after-school trips. Parents and community volunteers will facilitate the visits.

TASKS (ACTION DETAILS)

Goal 1: Student Motivation, Success, and Enjoyment

- Teachers to show career awareness video. (**All teachers by September 15; task accomplished.**)
- Teachers to administer interests/skills assessments. (**Lead teacher at each school site by November 1; task is on schedule.**)
- Teachers/aides/volunteers to match interest/skill test results for each student with career awareness choices to show education relevance. (**To be facilitated by classroom teachers for each student by December 1; task is on schedule.**)

- District language and math assessments to be administered for each student. **(Each teacher to complete by October 15; task accomplished.)**

Goal 2: Academic Support

- District to develop screening and training program for volunteer classroom tutors. **(District training coordinator to complete by October 15; will be accomplished by November 1.)**

- Community volunteers to be used in after-school tutoring program. **(Individual teachers to coordinate from 3:00 to 4:00 p.m. on Mondays, Wednesdays, and Thursdays.)**

- Individual assessment to be conducted to gauge math and language skill mastery. **(Individual teachers to conduct weekly until skill is mastered. When skill is mastered, teachers to move students to next skill and level. Task is in progress and on track.)**

Goal 3: Learning Styles, Multimodal Instruction

- Learning style test to be administered to determine how each student best learns. **(Each teacher by October 15.)**

- State standards to be used as a baseline and comprise 90% of instruction. **(Site principal to inspect individual teacher lesson plans weekly to ensure compliance.)**

- Content to be taught in auditory, visual, and kinesthetic modes. **(Principal to inspect lesson plans weekly. Vice principal to observe individual teachers monthly.)**

- Computer lab programs to be used to reinforce content with individual students. **(Each teacher on Tuesdays and Thursdays in computer lab.)**

- Monthly tests to be administered to determine individual student content acquisition and establish new foundation. **(Each teacher to test by 15th of each month; adjust content and repeat monthly.)**

Goal 4: Community Connection

- Visits to local assisted-living facilities, businesses and museums to be scheduled. **(Site PTA president by September 30; task accomplished.)**
- Community visits. **(PTA/community volunteers monthly during after-school hours.)**
- Students to apply learning from community visits. **(Each teacher to assign writing assignment following a visit. Assignment to be based on state standards and to be accomplished within two days of the visit. Task is on target.)**

Abbreviated Weekly Rolling Agenda

Our final example is a shortened version of the Rolling Agenda for the Acme School District. It focuses on the tasks and actions that need to be executed. This version is handy for meetings because you can move quickly through the list and note necessary changes.

Abbreviated Weekly Rolling Agenda: Acme School District

September 8 Weekly Rolling Agenda

TASKS (ACTION DETAILS)

1. Career awareness video showing (Principal)
2. Interest/skill assessments (Lead teacher)
3. Matching interests/skills assessments to career awareness (Individual teachers)
4. Language/math assessments (Individual teachers)
5. Volunteer tutor training (District training coordinator)
6. Language/math skill mastery (Individual teachers, ongoing)
7. Learning style test (Individual teachers)
8. State standard baseline instruction adherence (Principal)
9. Instructional content variety adherence (Vice principal)
10. Computer lab frequency (Individual teachers)
11. Monthly skill mastery tests (Individual teachers)

12. Community visits (PTA president)

13. Application of community visits (Individual teachers)

Quick Reference

This chapter focused on practical ways to implement and execute an organization's mission and vision. All too often, the mission and key initiatives become lost in the day-to-day grind of departmental tasks. By following the format outlined in the Rolling Agenda, you can remind everyone of the organization's priorities in all activities. This will enhance your ability to execute key objectives and ultimately fulfill your organization's mission and goals. Whether you adopt the Rolling Agenda or some variation, you must use a methodical tool that allows you to manage and execute the initiatives that are a priority to your executive leadership.

Setting Goals Based on the Mission and Vision

- Goals should be broken down into achievable plans, tasks, and actions and have specific relevance to the mission.
- Each task ought to have clearly defined roles and time frames associated with it.
- The goal-setting process should include autonomy and authority for team members to carry out the mission in their individual tasks.
- Once key tasks are completed or goals are achieved, take the time to recognize and celebrate accomplishments, especially of those who are relatively new to the organization.

Planning to Achieve Goals

- Strategically devised plans and their subsequent execution determine your success in reaching the goals you set.
- You need to assess risk and the amount of organizational change associated with a plan before it is enacted so you can determine how quickly the plan will become effective.
- Strategically adjusting a plan without overanalyzing is a delicate balancing act.

Developing Tasks to Execute Plans

- Without strategic execution, the best laid plans are useless.
- The ability to execute a plan is based on categorizing the key elements into achievable tasks.
- Tasks should always be assigned to those who have previously shown the ability to accomplish them or who have demonstrated the aptitude for increased responsibility.
- Getting individuals to buy in during the assignment of tasks is critical to the successful execution of plans and achievement of goals.

Completing Tasks

- Once tasks are assigned, you must inspect and measure them until they are complete.
- If you do not create a sense of urgency, tasks will roll from week to week, month to month, and even year to year.
- Actions are the steps needed to accomplish a task.
- Action execution leads to task completion, which leads to the execution of plans and the fulfillment of goals.
- When all team members are accomplishing their individual tasks, the results will be amazing.

Using Rolling Agendas

- The rolling agenda is a one- to two-page document that organizes and simplifies the execution process.
- The Rolling Agenda enables you to consistently keep the organization's mission and goals in the forefront of all communication to your team.
- The focus should be on the tasks and action details. These items form the benchmark for execution.
- Weekly sessions enable you to highlight accomplishments, create urgency, and adjust tasks and plans when necessary.

CHAPTER 5

Using Tactical
Management Skills

T HIS CHAPTER WILL examine the tactical management skills
managers need to develop. To be successful, you must organize
the strategic goals appropriately and advance toward them by using a
repeatable process. In other words, you need to establish a system of
procedures to ensure ongoing effectiveness.

Tactical management is focused on execution and is comprised of
small-scale tasks and actions executed to serve a larger purpose and
accomplish larger end goals. The tactical management areas addressed
in this chapter are organization and planning, delegation, preparation,
decision making, and remote management. You'll also learn techniques
for managing messages from your superiors to your subordinates and
for adjusting plans when they are not working well.

Organization and Planning

Having the ability to organize and devise plans and then execute them is the number one priority for a manager. Good managers
approach every expectation and challenge strategically to devise a plan
to best execute the organization's objectives. They organize the task at
hand and formulate a plan based on the human and material resources

that are available to them. They plan how to scale these resources properly and provide consistent empowerment, communication, and course adjustment to team members.

As mentioned in the "Vision" section in chapter 3, leaders must have the ability to anticipate. As they organize and devise a plan, they must see the desired result far in advance of others and be able to communicate it to the team members in a tangible way. Good managers must also anticipate challenges and obstacles to a plan and formulate solutions and adjustments before the challenges arise. They need to consistently stay ahead of the team and have well-thought-out strategic adjustments in their back pocket that they can pull out if necessary.

Staying ahead of your team requires that you discipline yourself to retreat from the day-to-day grind and objectively assess how your plan is working. Executive managers typically develop three- to five-year plans for their organizations to execute. For other managers, having a solid annual plan and being able to stay four to six weeks ahead of the team is sufficient. Failure to stay ahead of the team and make any needed adjustments will result in confusion. Confusion can lead to an erosion of trust, credibility, and respect, which can be reestablished only by executing goals.

When organizing an annual plan, try working from the end goal backward. The annual plan should be well thought out and have executable tasks and metrics aligned with the organization's mission and goals. Use the annual plan to create quarterly plans, monthly plans, and weekly plans that are all interrelated and build upon one another. The interrelation of the plans will enable you to develop agendas, tasks, and meetings that directly correlate to the organization's mission and goals.

Managers have to develop the skill of handling many items simultaneously and keeping their priorities straight. They must be able to organize many activities and implement multiple plans simultaneously. If managers get too bogged down in the details of noncritical goals or tasks, they will not be able to execute key initiatives.

This is where the Rolling Agenda can really help. It gives you the requisite structure necessary to jump between plans quickly in an organized manner. It enables you to have key plans working simultaneously with proper prioritization and to handle large amounts of activity in an efficient manner. Regardless of your experience level, it is difficult to effectively manage multiple key initiatives without proper organization and structure.

Structure refers to the ability to locate information quickly and reacquaint yourself with the intricacies of key goals and plans. Having this ability allows you to quickly reinforce or adjust a plan. Without structure, you'll find it extremely difficult to communicate multiple objectives to a team properly. The Rolling Agenda is helpful because it provides a solid, interrelated structure from which to launch multiple plans and execute the related tasks that lead to success.

Strategies for prioritization are a critical and necessary part of your tactical skills. Without constant reprioritization, you will be bogged down in daily activities that do not yield productive results. Your appointments, meetings, and to-do list have to relate to accomplishing key goals or they are simply wasted energy. You cannot merely hope that tomorrow will be less busy or present fewer challenges. You have to develop the ability to handle activity in an organized manner or you will fail. Constant reprioritization and adjustment will keep your eyes focused on what is really important. The tyranny of the urgent will not derail you from accomplishing your priorities.

Time management is also a critical skill. Time is the ultimate resource we have to accomplish what is important to us. Although you can organize and structure plans in many different ways, the only way to implement many plans simultaneously is to manage your time effectively.

Your daily tasks must relate directly to the organization's mission and goals. This presupposes that your time must be spent in fulfillment of those goals. This means you have to strip away tasks that do not directly relate to key initiatives.

Ideally, you will spend considerable time formulating a plan before it is launched. Hastily developed plans typically don't work. However, sometimes you will be under time pressure to launch a plan, and at such times you must make sure the fundamental bases are covered before taking action. You still need structure and organization, albeit in a compressed time frame.

There is no substitute for building consensus when developing and enacting a plan. This process will bring out fresh ideas from people with specific knowledge in particular areas. It will also create much-needed momentum when you are ready to present the plan to team members and launch it. For momentum to continue to build, you ultimately must instill confidence in the group that the plan will succeed.

Delegation

One of the most difficult tactical management techniques to learn is delegation. Most managers had been successful in their fields as individual contributors and then were promoted to management. They have certain standards for personal motivation and performance based on their own success. When they have to delegate activities, they often become frustrated because their subordinates do not perform to these standards. Some managers react by taking back the delegated tasks and performing them themselves. When they do so, the tasks may be done to their satisfaction, but the subordinates do not learn how to do the tasks well. Only after repeated attempts will team members gain the experience to execute the tasks to the desired standards. Your subordinates may never develop the ability to execute the tasks as well as you, but their ability to do them satisfactorily will enable you to focus on more strategic goals and plans.

Managers who cannot delegate effectively create a huge problem because they cannot scale their department or organization. They rely too much on themselves to execute the activities required to reach the organization's goals.

You must teach, train, motivate, and mentor your team members to enhance their skill sets. If necessary, micromanage initially but then loosen the reins as people's skills improve. Be patient in the early stages so you do not discourage anyone. The results may not be what you could have produced yourself, but keep in mind that you are trying to enable others to master a task or skill so that you can move on to bigger initiatives. Proper delegation, supervision, and coaching will enable you to more effectively manage your personal time and grow the department and organization successfully. A subordinate may be only 80 percent as effective as you in accomplishing a task, but 80 percent spread across a broad range of goals and tasks will enable great growth.

Delegation is more art than science, and good managers will be able to delegate activities as their team members gain skill and experience. You need to know the strengths of your team members so you know which tasks to delegate to whom to ensure success. Start with smaller, less complex tasks and gradually assign larger and more complex activities as team members prove their ability to execute them.

To see how effective delegation works, let's return to the Acme School District. This scenario exemplifies delegation at a number of management levels. The superintendent has ultimate responsibility for accomplishing the mission of developing lifelong learners who flourish in their individual learning styles and are connected to the community. The superintendent motivates the individual school site principals to buy into the mission and delegates the execution of key goals and plans to them. The principals are responsible for the goals of sustaining student motivation, enhancing academic support systems, applying content and multimodal instruction, and connecting students to the community. To achieve these goals, the principals need to effectively delegate tasks and responsibilities to their resources, including a district training coordinator, vice principals, lead teachers, individual classroom teachers, Parent-Teacher Association (PTA) presidents, and community volunteers.

For the goal of sustaining student motivation, one principal (Greg) has delegated the task of managing the interest/skill assessments to the school's lead teacher. He feels confident delegating this task because the lead teacher has the requisite experience and shows the leadership, attitude, and aptitude to execute it. Individual classroom teachers are responsible for showing the career awareness video and administering the required assessments for math, language, and interests/skills. Classroom teachers will in turn manage and delegate the administrative tasks of matching assessment results to aides and volunteers. Once this task is complete, teachers can then correlate the assessment results with potential career choices and show their students how their studies apply to their futures. By delegating tasks that match skill sets and experience, the principal has increased his ability to achieve the district's goals more quickly.

The goal of enhancing academic support for the students is a complex one to accomplish. To properly address it, the principal will rely on a district coordinator to screen and train prospective volunteers. The principal has chosen to delegate this task to the district coordinator so that proper guidelines are followed and risk issues associated with the screening process are minimized. The task of recruiting volunteers for academic support falls on the classroom teachers, who will refer candidates to the district coordinator for screening and training before the volunteers enter the classroom.

The goal of multimodal instruction involves close inspection of lesson plans and classroom instruction. This requires the skills possessed by experienced school administrators. Because of the strategic nature of this goal, the principal has decided to allocate time to review all lesson plans himself weekly. He will then communicate the appropriate adjustments to each teacher directly. All information pertaining to lesson plan review and adjustment will be communicated to the vice principal, who will do the classroom observations and ensure lesson plans are implemented to district standards. The vice principal will also be tasked with the performance coaching of individual teachers and report back to the principal.

For community connection, the principal will rely on the PTA president and classroom teachers to accomplish the goal. The principal has determined that the PTA has many people who want to help. By directing them to specific tasks he will be using them productively and expanding community connections at the same time. Because the PTA is a volunteer organization, the principal will have to allocate sufficient time to communicate and evaluate the progress of the tasks that have been delegated to the PTA president. He has decided this task is important enough that he needs to manage it directly.

In the LGLO example, the manager (Karen) has responsibility to accomplish the mission of helping people physically, educationally, and socially in a profitable manner. She must also focus on the key goals of customer satisfaction, positive store environment, employee motivation and compensation, risk-reward scenarios, and community involvement. All of the tasks necessary to accomplish these goals are important, but Karen cannot do everything by herself. Her human resources include Joe, who is an assistant manager, and Chad, who is an hourly employee.

Relative to the customer satisfaction goal, Karen has chosen to retain the mailer task herself as she deems it to be strategic and wants to evaluate its effectiveness firsthand. She has delegated measurement of the repeat/referral business to Joe as he has the experience and systems expertise to manage the ongoing process. Chad is relatively new;

therefore, Karen will delegate simple tasks, such as maintaining the store environment, to him.

As a manager, Karen will evaluate daily employee performance, employee compensation, risk-related tasks, and community involvement. Because the task is so strategic, Karen has also chosen to visit and develop contact with the top ten diabetic Medicare doctors in the area. The task of visiting fifty local doctors and the twenty-five physical therapists is large, so Karen will delegate the majority of the effort to Joe. She will oversee the program for the top five in each category to make sure the message is delivered properly and to give herself the opportunity to evaluate the program directly. Karen has enough confidence in Joe to delegate the remaining sixty-five visits to him. This will help develop Joe's skill set, minimize overall organizational risk, and take part of the load off Karen.

The delegation choices Karen has made are strategic to LGLO's mission, goals, and plans. By prioritizing tasks and assigning them to the proper people, Karen can focus on the most important initiatives. Her delegation enables her to achieve the key objectives of employee skill development and also affords her the ability to grow and scale the store effectively.

Hopefully, these examples have been helpful in illustrating the flow and thought process of delegation. Good managers always keep the strategic big picture in mind and see how the execution of administrative tasks can build a foundation to accomplish key plans and goals.

Preparation

Nothing sets apart a good manager (or anyone, for that matter) more than consistent preparation. We all have had experiences when we have prepared thoroughly and seen the positive results. Conversely, we have all had experiences when we did not have enough time or we lacked the discipline to prepare and suffered the consequences. When a manager exhibits thorough preparation and presents a plan or task to either superiors or subordinates, the audience sees the value and importance of it. They know that the manager has taken the task seriously and wants to execute it successfully. As stated earlier, the most important resource we have is time, and using it in thorough preparation will yield positive outcomes.

Proper preparation is actually easier to achieve now than in the past. An abundance of information is available instantaneously on the Internet. In preparation for meetings with another organization, you can access websites to familiarize yourself with that organization's mission and goals. You can find press releases, executive biographies, financial data, organizational structures, and so on to quickly familiarize yourself with the organization and make your interactions more meaningful. When preparing for internal meetings or activities, look at both personal initiatives as well as organizational initiatives and assess how you are progressing to accomplish those plans.

Whether you're preparing for internal or external organizational conversations, strive to become an expert in your chosen field. You should bring value to those you interact with. You can gain expertise in your field through a variety of resources, including industry magazines, group organizations, and your personal network both internal and external to your organization. Preparation goes beyond just being ready for a meeting or lesson; it entails going the extra distance to learn about your field in detail so you can bring insight, value, and expertise to others.

Decision Making

Decision making spans the spectrum from major plan adjustments to minor task tweaks. All decisions need to be made in line with an organization's mission, goals, plans, and objectives. A short-term decision that does not take into consideration long-term goals may lead to wasted time and resources.

Good managers always make decisions that are in the best interest of the organization, not their own personal interests. If you consistently make decisions in the best interest of the organization as a whole, your work will be recognized and your career aspirations will be realized.

Approach every decision as if it were being made by an executive of an organization. Try to think like the chief executive about resources and personnel and guide your decisions accordingly. This mini-CEO approach will ensure that your short-term decisions fall in line with long-term organizational objectives.

Even if you need to make a decision quickly, you must assimilate as much input as possible to make an informed judgment. Seek this input from both subordinates and superiors. Brainstorming sessions are an excellent way to bring forth necessary ideas that can help with decision making.

Management is ultimately about execution and requires situation analysis skills to ensure positive results. If you prepare properly by anticipating how circumstances will unfold, you will be ready when a challenge arises and you can make an informed, quick decision. In addition, you can more readily communicate solutions clearly to team members who will be able to carry out their responsibilities in quick order.

Keeping perspective when making a decision is critical. Your ability to face a challenge, devise a solution, and make a decision without getting overwhelmed is a sign of emotional strength. Stay focused on making the decision at hand and don't get caught up in potential scenarios that may never happen or are irrelevant to the situation. When making big decisions, make them calmly and with confidence. Remember that when the heat is turned up, exceptional leaders are at their best.

In the Acme School District, managers at all levels work within a defined organizational structure. The hierarchy consists of a district superintendent, school site principals, vice principals, district training coordinators, lead teachers, classroom teachers, students, and volunteers. Each manager is called upon to make decisions within the district framework. Because many tiers are involved in plan execution, upper-level decision makers must be intimately attuned to the progress of their plans. Their plan adjustments need to be very deliberate and thoroughly researched because the slightest tweaks could have far-reaching impacts that cause initiatives to be delayed or compromised.

Regardless of the size of an organization, the task-action foundational approach can be used. In the case of Acme, the principals and classroom teachers are the key elements in achieving the district's mission and goals. Acme's executive management team members, including the school board, superintendent, and principals, have decided on a direction for the district and agree that its culture can be established only through enacting the agreed-upon plans.

In devising these Acme plans, principals made the decision to cover less content in their academic curricula. They put their academic focus on state standards, thereby freeing up time for classroom teachers to promote relevance, skill mastery, and motivation toward lifelong learning.

Acme decision makers have thoroughly researched and devised plans to meet the district's goals. They have decided that the principals must be the primary proponents of the mission and also participate in its implementation via weekly inspections of teacher lesson plans and coordination of volunteer resources to execute key tasks. Vice principals are assigned classroom evaluation and teacher coaching to ensure initiatives such as interest assessments, skill mastery, learning style assessments, and method variety are accomplished. Lead teachers are tasked with assisting classroom teachers with interest assessments, skill mastery assessments, and compliance with state standards. Both the vice principals and lead teachers have to focus on motivating classroom teachers to personally own the district goals and manage their adoption in the classroom. In addition, they must make sure to give classroom teachers the autonomy to adapt their implementation to their unique sets of students.

Classroom teachers are the ultimate managers for the district's goal and plan implementation. They must decide how to best execute their given tasks in the classroom environment. Their decision-making process must include lesson planning, which prioritizes the key initiatives of assessments, skill mastery, and methodology varieties focused on state standard content.

Finally, the superintendent and principals have decided that to truly promote Acme's mission and goals they must be directly involved in the community. The principal's task of interfacing directly with PTA management and community volunteers is vital, so the school board approved it, even though it takes away from some of the principal's school site time. All these decisions were made in the best interest of achieving Acme's mission and goals.

At LGLO, large-scale planning and decision making carries a great deal of risk. Because the store is a small three-person operation, the owner must constantly assess both positive and negative risk scenarios. He has to be in constant communication with the store manager to make sure she is content and motivated and carrying out the mission and goals. He must also be ready with an adequate succession plan should the manager leave for any reason. He must decide if the assistant manager can be promoted or if he must look outside the organization.

The LGLO manager's decision making revolves around putting the right people on the right tasks to ensure success. Managers have to help team members gain experience by building upon the specific tasks being executed. This bottom-up approach enables plans to be accomplished effectively within the prescribed time frames. Decision making in this context equates to staff skill assessment and task assignment. The store manager, Karen, has decided to retain certain tasks herself while maintaining oversight of all delegated assignments.

Administratively, Karen feels good about the plans, tasks, and actions she has developed. She has decided to assign Joe and Chad tasks that fit their skill sets. Joe has been given a few critical tasks, such as assessing repeat business and visiting doctors. Karen will need to monitor Joe's progress by both speaking with him and calling key doctors to judge his effectiveness. She has assigned Chad more entry-level duties, such as maintaining the store environment and sending mailers. If the tasks are not being executed to Karen's expectations, she must decide which adjustments should be made to both personnel and tasks. By focusing on tasks/actions and plans, she can minimize subjectivity and center communication with her staff on expectations. Karen's daily decisions and adjustments provide the critical framework within which key LGLO initiatives are accomplished.

Management involves making a series of proper judgments, course corrections, and adjustments to achieve an organization's goals. The examples in this section have shown the thought process behind Acme's and LGLO's decisions.

Remote Management

As technology advances and team members become more geographically dispersed, we are faced with new demands as managers. Managing virtual teams and individuals is becoming more commonplace.

Whether managing a remote team or having a one-on-one session, the same management skills apply. When conducting virtual discussions, however, it is even more important to provide definitive structure and organization. The agenda becomes the preeminent point of focus and reference, much more so than the speaker. Whereas in-person meetings allow a manager to maintain eye contact and direct conversations in a fluid manner, in remote meetings, discussions tend to unfold in starts and stops because the participants can have difficulty with conversational flow. For this reason, the agenda needs to be extremely tight and focused only on key points.

In remote settings, it is very easy to lose the attention of your audience. You must stress an environment of engagement for the participants. For example, call on team members individually for feedback on specific agenda items to keep them engaged. Effective facilitation of remote meetings also requires you to move quickly between topics and inputs from team members. If you get bogged down on any topic or feedback item, you risk losing people's attention.

At all times, try to simulate an in-person session as much as possible using available technology tools. Computer-based collaboration tools are becoming more affordable and enhanced voice and document-sharing tools are great aides for conducting remote meetings. Videoconferencing is also excellent for remote meetings; however, poor video quality can quickly compromise a meeting's objectives. Regardless of which technologies you use, make sure they work properly and participants are adequately trained. Technology training, adoption, and usage are essential to effective remote meetings. If you spend half a session merely getting participants online, valuable meeting time is wasted and the technology tools are useless.

Those who have experience conducting remote sessions can attest to their inherent frustration. Managers can *feel* the lack of participant attention through questions like "Can you repeat that?" or "What was that?" You can address this lack of attention in two ways. The first is to stay patient and repeat yourself. The second approach is to simply skip past the participant and call the next person's name. This will let the team know that attention lapses are not appreciated. Try varying these approaches when addressing this issue.

Effectively managing remote team or individual sessions requires discipline from both the manager and the participants. In the virtual environment, the leader has to take a more commanding approach and handle agenda items quickly. Communication is much more difficult than with in-person meetings and requires a more directed approach to addressing agenda items and requesting feedback.

Management Messaging

At any level of management, you must decide how to communicate the messages you receive from your superiors to your team. You need to deliver directives to your subordinates in a way that will motivate them. Passing along a message as is can be counterproductive. Your team's perception will be that you do not own the message yourself and they may discount its importance. Instead you need to extract the key points of the message and deliver them with actionable goals and tasks relevant to the team members.

Messages from executives are often targeted at managers and not individual contributors, so you need to edit them for distribution. As a manager you have to realize that a great deal of the information you receive is not appropriate to share verbatim. You are often entrusted with confidential information that needs to remain with you only. Disclosing this information not only is unethical but also can lead to needless speculation and gossip among team members.

Keep your team focused on executing the goals and plans you have laid out. Don't bother them with information that cannot be acted upon. Burdening the team with speculation or management-level scenarios may distract them from meeting their individual expectations.

People in middle management positions often feel like they are being pressured from above and below. If you're in middle management, be sure you allow only the very important information to "spill over" to the team. Be cognizant of shielding those under you from information they really don't need to know. Your primary responsibility is to keep your team focused on executing their objectives.

Adjusting Plans for Greater Effectiveness

Not every plan is going to work in its initial iteration. When a plan is not working at maximum effectiveness, don't be afraid to reexamine the goals, simplify the plan, and reorganize it to increase the chances of efficient execution. The process is also helpful when you are taking on a big project or faced with new circumstances or added complexities on an existing undertaking.

This process helps you step back, reassess how matters are unfolding, and make the necessary adjustments in an organized manner without knee-jerk reactions. It is a back-to-basics approach that enables you and the team to tighten your focus. Begin by reexamining the goals. Simplify the plan by organizing it around only the most essential objectives. Then adapt the plan and make it easily understood by your team. The revised plan should be simple to follow, manage, and execute. Once you are able to get a goal back on track, you can add plans and continue to build on them. By refocusing, simplifying, and executing, you will revitalize the team's momentum and build the confidence needed to achieve organizational priorities.

Let's look at an example of how the Acme School District used this process. One of the district's goals is to use a variety of methodologies and teaching styles to best serve students of all learning styles. Acme wants to use auditory, visual, and kinesthetic modes to teach students. It also wants to use state-standards-based content with a technology emphasis and to assess students after each unit to make sure they are mastering the content before moving to the next skill level.

When the Acme School District administrators reexamined this goal, they determined that they were achieving some of it but falling short in other areas. Their plan to achieve this goal had five elements, which they examine relative to execution:

- Element 1 was to determine how each student best learns. The administrators felt they were doing well in achieving this part of the plan because their learning style assessment tests correlated to what the teachers observed with each student.

- Element 2 was to ensure that the state standard curriculum comprised 90 percent of all instruction. This is a district mandate and cannot be adjusted.

- Element 3 of the plan was to teach all content in auditory, visual, and kinesthetic modes. Acme administrators felt they were not effectively addressing the needs of students who possess a kinesthetic learning style. There were a number of reasons for this. First, the available kinesthetic curriculum was very limited. Second, the district had asked the teachers to look for their own resources to address the kinesthetic learning style. Because the teachers had so many other demands on their time, this had been difficult for them to do. Third, fewer students have this learning style, so it had become a lower priority.

- Element 4 of the plan was to use technology to reinforce content with individual students. This had proven difficult to achieve due to logistical challenges and a lack of computer resources.
- Element 5 was to administer tests to determine all students' content acquisition and ability to move to the next step in their education. Acme administrators felt they were doing a good job with individual student assessment and that no students were moving to another level before they were ready. This element of the plan is a foundation goal of the district.

Next, Acme tried to simplify the plan. Elements 1, 2, and 5 could not be changed per district mandate. The administrators felt they were satisfactorily executing their plan to achieve the goals in these areas. They determined that the key initiative they were not accomplishing was the provision of resources and teaching to students who have a kinesthetic learning style. They also determined that utilizing computers to reinforce learning was not working due to resource constraints and logistical issues.

To simplify their plan, Acme administrators chose to make two adjustments: they dropped the technology element for now and will concentrate on the kinesthetic learning issues. They will address this in three ways. First, the district will prioritize the acquisition of kinesthetic learning style resources. Second, instead of having individual teachers look for materials, district personnel will research and acquire a kinesthetic learning style curriculum for each grade level. They will make sure the curriculum meets state standards. They will then train each teacher in the application of the curriculum. Finally, Acme principals will closely inspect lesson plans and observe teachers to make sure they are giving ample time in the classrooms to teach students with the kinesthetic learning style.

Acme simplified the original plan by eliminating the technology element and taking district control of the kinesthetic learning style issue. The revised plan will be communicated to all district personnel by revising the Rolling Agenda to reflect the changes. The Rolling Agenda will provide the organization with a focus document for the newly adjusted district plan. The adapted plan is simpler to manage and execute and focuses on the key goals of the district.

Reexamining the goals, simplifying the plan, and reorganizing the Rolling Agenda provides an effective means of management and gives an organization the ability to execute tasks efficiently. It reflects the continuous process of prioritizing, adjusting, and adapting plans to ensure execution of the organization's mission.

Quick Reference

If you want to succeed as a manager, you need to organize strategic goals appropriately and advance toward them by using a repeatable process. Tactical management is focused on execution and is comprised of small-scale tasks and actions completed to serve a larger purpose and accomplish larger end goals.

Organization and Planning

- Staying ahead of your team requires that you discipline yourself to retreat from the day-to-day grind and objectively assess how your plan is working.
- When organizing an annual plan, work backward from the end goal.
- If you don't constantly reprioritize, you will be bogged down in daily activities that do not yield productive results.
- The only way to implement many plans simultaneously is to manage your time effectively.

Delegation

- Managers who cannot delegate effectively create huge problems because their department or organization cannot grow and scale properly.
- Subordinates may never develop the ability to execute a task as well as you can, but their ability to do it satisfactorily will enable you to focus on more strategic goals and plans.
- When delegating, start with smaller, simpler tasks and gradually assign larger and more complex activities as team members prove their ability to execute them.

Preparation

- Nothing sets apart a good manager more than consistent preparation.
- If you prepare thoroughly, your superiors and subordinates will notice.
- You need to strive to become an expert in your field so you can bring insight, value, and expertise to others.

Decision Making

- If you consistently make decisions in the best interest of the organization as a whole, your career will benefit too.
- A good approach is to try to think like the CEO about resources and personnel.
- To make an informed decision, you should always assimilate as much input as possible, even if time is short.
- You need to stay focused on making the decision at hand and not get caught up in potential scenarios that may never happen or are irrelevant to the situation.

Remote Management

- The same management skills you use with on-site teams are needed when you are managing a remote team. You should try to simulate in-person discussions as much as possible.
- Virtual discussions require even more structure and organization than in-person meetings.
- In remote meetings the agenda becomes more important than the speaker. You need to take command and handle agenda items quickly.
- Calling on team members individually for feedback on specific agenda items will keep them engaged.

Management Messaging

- When top management issues directives, you need to give them to your subordinates in a motivational manner.

- Extract the key points of a message and deliver them with actionable goals and tasks relevant to team members.
- Middle managers should allow only the very important information to "spill over" to their team and shield those under them from information they really don't need to know.

Adjusting Plans for Greater Effectiveness

- Effective management is the continuous process of prioritizing, adjusting, and adapting plans to ensure execution of the organization's mission and goals.
- When a plan is not working well, it's time to reexamine the goals, simplify the plan, and reorganize it to increase the chances of efficient execution.
- The process of reexamining goals and simplifying a plan is also helpful when you are taking on a big project or faced with new circumstances or added complexities on an existing undertaking.
- By refocusing, simplifying, and executing, you will revitalize the momentum and give team members the confidence they need.
- Reexamine, simplify, and organize your goals around only the most essential objectives. Then adapt your plan and make it easily understood by your team using a revised rolling agenda.

CHAPTER 6

Developing Your Team

IN THIS CHAPTER, we will examine how you can develop the critical elements of camaraderie and chemistry among team members so your organization can achieve high goals. People tend to be individualistic, and developing a willingness to achieve common goals is sometimes difficult to do. Because many people are wired to look only at their own priorities and are unwilling to make sacrifices to achieve a greater purpose, good leaders and managers have to develop a team atmosphere. Teams working together will always yield greater results than individuals working on their own.

The foundational tenet of teamwork is that at some time, an individual will have to sacrifice something for the good of the group. To develop strong teams, you need to consider environment, rhythm, questioning and brainstorming techniques, team meeting facilitation, and overall teamwork.

Environment

Your job as a manager is to create an environment where people can flourish. Creating this environment requires trust, respect, and credibility. Trust is critical to leadership and is reflected in a leader's character. Respect is tied to trust and comes from making good decisions and relating to people in a professional and empathetic manner. Credibility is tied to respect and is earned with a pattern of successes and recognition of those successes.

Setting an example for desired behaviors is also critical for creating a team environment. If you consistently make decisions in the best interest of the group, you model teamwork, and this becomes a standard mode of operation.

To create the requisite team environment, you must create an environment with positive energy and enthusiasm. This means that you must minimize your negative comments when you're with the group, even if you need to withdraw when you encounter frustrating situations so you don't say something you may regret. Show genuine enthusiasm for accomplishing the organization's mission and goals and consistently project a positive attitude because you set the tone. Remember that positive momentum is created when tasks are accomplished and good results are attained. When positive momentum is created, people want to contribute and a team environment is better established.

A team environment is also created by establishing an open and nonthreatening atmosphere. Continually ask people what they think of ideas to promote an environment where they give genuine input and feedback.

Good team environments nurture positive relationships and allow for give and take. All team members must feel they are contributing or discord can occur. People work better when they connect with one another and get along. To create a setting that fosters good relationships, you will need to monitor both the relationships within the group and the overall team environment.

Rhythm

Getting the team into a consistent rhythm is vital to achieving goals because team members need to know what to expect. To establish a healthy rhythm, be consistent about meetings and scheduling. Weekly team meetings are useful to reinforce key short-term initiatives, measure results, assess progress, and make appropriate adjustments. The specific content of the meetings could include growth results, forecasts, progress toward goals, input from team members, calendar events, and training. These meetings can be conducted in person or over the phone if the team is geographically dispersed. In addition to measuring short-term progress, use the weekly meetings to frame and reinforce organizational mission and goals, remembering to always relate the weekly tasks to the big picture.

Monthly, quarterly, and individual meetings should have a consistent rhythm as well. Try to avoid cancellation at all costs. Monthly and quarterly reviews are fundamental in communicating with and coaching team members.

Scheduling weekly, monthly, and quarterly meetings will prevent the event-oriented mind-set that occurs when team members do not know what to expect and meetings are sporadic or called at the last minute. If you are not organized and can't stay ninety days ahead, the team cannot get into a rhythm and poor performance will typically result. The result is a reactive culture, and as previously mentioned, reactive organizations cannot meet their goals over time. Similarly, reactive departments have difficulty completing tasks and achieving goals if scheduling is choppy and not rhythmic.

In addition to having team meetings, touch base with individual team members frequently to reinforce key objectives and tasks. Schedule short sessions with individuals early in the week to get insight into their individual objectives and tasks, specific weekly priorities, and so on. Focus on individual motivation, strength areas, areas of concern, and overall performance. Be specific if performance improvement is needed and use the time to build a relational partnership with the individual. Remember to use leadership techniques to communicate that you are interested in the person's success and that you are a resource to help him or her achieve it.

You can also use weekly individual sessions to reset expectations and make the appropriate adjustments if you think a team member is straying off course. These brief sessions are great for relationship development and will ensure that all team members are buying into the organizational goals and the overall team concept. They establish a quick-paced rhythm for your organization.

Establishing individual and team rhythm is a key to building a strong organization. If situations arise that necessitate changing team or individual meetings, make sure to communicate the changes to team members as far in advance as possible. This will show that you value your team members' time and also reinforce that you are thinking ahead. Finally, if you sense that weekly meetings are getting stale or repetitive, feel free to skip them occasionally to change the pattern. However, monthly and quarterly reviews should always proceed as scheduled because they provide much-needed time to assess performance and coach individuals toward success.

Questioning and Brainstorming Techniques

Another key skill is the ability to ask pertinent questions that uncover creative ideas and facilitate learning in those you manage. Learning takes place when individuals are motivated and take ownership of the subject matter at hand. Your ability to promote an open questioning process enables valuable inputs to take place.

To communicate effectively, oftentimes you must say something in a variety of ways to facilitate understanding. Using questions can orient the group to key goals and help them understand why the goals are important. To maximize the process, you need to present content and garner feedback in creative and innovative ways.

Good questioning techniques require active listening and follow-up so you can chip away at anything that hinders people's understanding of a goal or plan. Only by active listening can you understand exactly how well people comprehend your message. Active listening simply means restating the key elements of what a person is saying to confirm your understanding. It also shows you value those participating in the discussion.

To illustrate the techniques of good questioning and active listening, we'll use the Acme School District as an example. Principal Greg is discussing an academic support goal with teacher Donna. Greg asks questions in a variety of ways to facilitate both his and Donna's understanding of the issues. He uses active listening to make sure they are communicating effectively. See how the confirmations and techniques of active listening help to build mutual understanding in the conversation.

GREG: Donna, how is it going using the ten secondary school students as tutors?

DONNA: Not very well, Greg. They don't show up at all sometimes, and the ones who do are often late.

GREG: So they don't show up and some are late, is that correct? Have you found any of them to be reliable and helpful?

DONNA: Yes, there are three tutors that are dependable.

GREG: Three of them are helpful? Who are they? Can we really depend on them?

DONNA: Yes, we can depend on Rosa, Marcus, and Sam. The kids love them too.

GREG: How about we match Rosa, Marcus, and Sam to some of our students who need extra help?

DONNA: That would be great, but we still have some other students who need help.

GREG: I understand, Donna. I know we have a lot of students who need help. But it sounds like we can count on only these three tutors. Can you pick the six students who need the most help so we can match the three tutors with them next week? We can continue to recruit tutors and hope to find more like Rosa, Marcus, and Sam.

Like questioning techniques, brainstorming techniques are essential to management skill. Brainstorming is a group process that involves the spontaneous contribution of ideas. Brainstorming sessions bring out fresh and much-needed ideas that you can implement to attain goals and carry out plans effectively.

To facilitate a brainstorming session, you need to define the goals, problems, or initiatives to be addressed in detail and in writing for all to view. State the desired input in specific terms so the session does not get sidetracked. Begin the session by presenting a list of ideas you have formulated to initiate feedback. Explain that all ideas are welcome but will not necessarily be implemented. This way, people will not be discouraged or demotivated if their ideas are not utilized. Express that you value each idea and the person who suggests it.

Immediately quash any negative comments about an idea or person. Then reset the tone by repeating that all thoughts are welcome and that there are no right or wrong suggestions. Do this regardless of the stature of the individual who gives the negative input. If you are not diligent in suppressing negativity during a brainstorming session, it can quickly get out of control. By insisting on a positive environment free from criticism, you can promote productive brainstorming sessions.

The sessions should be characterized by open-mindedness, and team members should be encouraged to think out of the box. Byproducts of good brainstorming sessions are the bonding of team members and the laying of a foundation for the execution of key organizational goals and plans.

Conclude every session with a summary of ideas, referring to ideas from each team member who participated. Thank team members for their time and participation. Regardless of which ideas you decide to write into a plan, you can take solace in the fact that you have done your due diligence by seeking inputs from all parties. Even if their ideas are not implemented, most team members will appreciate the fact that they have been asked for input. By conducting brainstorming sessions properly, you can create momentum when the ultimate plan or solution is presented to the group and subsequently launched.

The following examples illustrate Acme and LGLO questioning and brainstorming techniques. They also show the sequential thought process and structure involved.

Questioning and Brainstorming Techniques: Acme School District

The following questioning and brainstorming techniques revolve around Acme's mission, goals, plans, tasks, and actions. All sessions should end with a verbal summary and the promise to give a written summary of ideas to all participants the next day or sooner, if possible.

EXAMPLE 1

The school site principal wants teachers to be more attuned to the school district's mission of developing lifelong learners who can pursue academic achievement in their individual learning styles and are connected to the community. He uses the following open-ended and closed-ended questions. With either type of question, the principal makes it a habit to call on peer leaders to initiate the discussion. He never hesitates to call on people for their input because silence is the worst possible scenario in brainstorming sessions.

1. What do you think you are doing well in your planning and instruction to help achieve the mission? (Closed)

2. What additional actions do you think you could be taking? (Closed)

3. Let's go around the room and have each teacher share a best practice that helps achieve the mission. (Closed)

4. Do you feel that you personally are a lifelong learner? How so? (Open)

5. As a teacher who continues to learn, what are your best learning styles? (Closed)

6. What are some ideas you are presently using to connect your students to the community? (Closed)

In this example, the principal is attempting to get teachers to own the district's mission individually through open- and closed-ended questions. He is also subtly communicating that adherence to the mission is nonnegotiable and that all teachers must find ways to achieve it in their classrooms. The questions in this brainstorming example bring out many tangible ideas that can be implemented to better promote the Acme School District's mission.

EXAMPLE 2

This brainstorming session relates to a lack of teacher effort in executing Acme's goal of providing an academic support system that enables students to succeed to the best of their abilities. The principal asks the following questions to get everyone to share ideas on how this goal can better be accomplished.

1. Why do you think we are struggling to achieve this goal? (Open)

2. Do you really believe that all of us inside and outside the education community are responsible for a child's education? (Closed)

3. What role should volunteers play in achieving our goal? (Open)

4. Which parents or other volunteers are involved in tutoring in your classroom and how effective are they? (Closed) What can we do to make them more effective? (Open)

5. Have you involved the PTA leadership in helping recruit tutoring volunteers? (Closed)

6. Which of you are successful at recruiting nonparent volunteers for the tutoring program, and how are you doing it? (Open)

7. I know how busy you are as teachers. How can you manage and delegate some of your tasks to help us reach our goal? (Closed)

8. What can I do to help you attain this goal? (Open)

In this example, the principal communicates that both he and the teachers have been negligent in achieving this goal by using terms like "our" and "we." Again, through his questioning the principal is implying that execution of the goal is nonnegotiable. It is a matter of finding ways to accomplish it, not *if* it will be accomplished. He also stresses the fact that the teachers don't necessarily have to accomplish it themselves but that they can develop delegation strategies to achieve it.

EXAMPLE 3

The following questions are for a brainstorming session where the principal is looking for best practices on how to better meet goal 3, which centers on learning styles, multimodal approaches, standards-based content, technology, and skill mastery.

1. After reviewing lesson plans and performing classroom observations, I think we are doing pretty well in executing our plan. How do you feel we are doing? (Open)

2. Do you think we are meeting all the students' needs with this approach? (Open)

3. How do you think we can improve kinesthetic learning? (Open)

4. Most education is dominated by auditory and visual learning approaches. What specific kinesthetic techniques are you using to connect with students who favor that learning style? (Closed)

5. Do you think the present state standard curriculum is effective in executing our plan? (Open)

6. Has anyone used supplemental materials to assist in achieving our plan? What are they? (Closed)

7. What can we do to reinforce learning through kinesthetic techniques? (Open)

8. How is the foundational skill mastery assessment going? (Open)

9. What can we do to improve it? (Closed)

In this example, the principal is seeking strictly best practice inputs because the group is executing the plan satisfactorily. In this context he is acting as a facilitator more than a manager and trying to uncover beneficial ideas. This type of brainstorming session is great for team bonding because the focus is not on a particular item that has to be improved. Typically, these types of best-practice-sharing sessions have a more relaxed, creative environment.

Questioning and Brainstorming Techniques: LGLO Specialty Shoe Store

The next set of examples comes from LGLO, a much smaller organization. The brainstorming meetings revolve around LGLO's mission, goals, plans, tasks, and actions. As in the previous examples, the manager uses both open- and closed-ended questions to address issues.

EXAMPLE 1

In this brainstorming meeting, the store manager wants to reinforce how important customer satisfaction is to LGLO. Her list of questions incorporates this goal as well as its accompanying plans, tasks and actions. She also incorporates tasks and actions from other goals that relate to the referral program because referrals and repeat business are a measure of customer satisfaction.

1. Our customer satisfaction is good, but we can always improve it. I know that you ask all customers about their experience. What are they saying about us? (Open; reinforces the needed focus and behavior of asking each customer)

2. How do you think we can increase customer satisfaction by improving our store environment? (Open)

3. How can we modify our five-question customer satisfaction mailer to better measure results? (Closed)

4. What type of feedback do you get when you phone customers as a follow-up to their store visit? (Closed)

5. Repeat customer business is a sign of a satisfied customer and is a huge source of revenue. What products or services do you think we can add to get our existing customers to visit the store more frequently? (Open)

6. How can we get more referrals from our customer base? (Open)

7. How can we get more referrals from local doctors? (Open)

8. What can you do individually to help improve customer satisfaction? (Closed)

The questions in this brainstorming session reinforce the importance of customer satisfaction as well as make sure each employee personally owns the goal. The questions also are intended to seek creative ideas for improvement relative to process, procedures, and the overall environment.

EXAMPLE 2

The store manager has to address a specific issue related to the goal of creating a store environment that rewards entrepreneurship, daily employee motivation, and teamwork in a highly ethical environment. The specific issues are teamwork and motivation. The manager's strategy is to begin with a brainstorming session followed by a one-on-one meeting with each employee to address individual concerns. She will then hold a team meeting in which she'll present managerial directives and initiatives. This example highlights a technique whereby the manager makes a directional statement before asking a question.

1. As you know, LGLO emphasizes teamwork and individual motivation in the store environment. Right now we are not meeting expectations. How do you think we are doing? (Open; frames the issues)

2. You all know our goal is for employees to go above and beyond their job descriptions and expectations. How do you think you are doing individually? (Closed)

3. You all know our LGLO goal for teamwork. The reason we emphasize teamwork is to promote a good working environment and because LGLO believes that in working together, we

can be exponentially more effective in accomplishing our goals. How do you think we can improve teamwork? (Open)

4. How are we doing handling multiple customers simultaneously and sharing the workload when the store is busy? How can we improve? (Open, then closed)

5. How are you doing relative to achieving your pedorthist certification? How do you plan to get your certification in the next six months? (Closed; relates to motivation)

6. We are presently not exceeding our sales targets, which hinders the ability of each of us to earn income. How can we increase sales? (Open)

This example has fewer and more pointed questions because the issues need to be framed properly and will be addressed in follow-up meetings. The questions place more emphasis on stating the issues than garnering creative input. However, asking the questions in a group format is beneficial so everyone leaves the brainstorming session with a common understanding of what needs to be achieved.

EXAMPLE 3

One of LGLO's goals is to become a part of the local community and contribute 10 percent of its annual profits to a local charity. LGLO management would like to have their employees extend the community involvement goal to each of their individual spheres of influence. The intent of this brainstorming session is to foster team bonding and extend employees' reach in their communities.

1. How are you each connecting to your community? (Open)

2. LGLO asks store managers like me to attend meetings of local service organizations, such as Rotary clubs, chambers of commerce, school Parent-Teacher Associations, and so on. Are any of you involved in organizations like that? (Closed)

3. Do any of you talk about LGLO and what we do in the community at school, your kids' activities, church, grocery stores, and so on? (Open)

4. I have had business cards made for each of you, so feel free to hand them out. Whom do you think you will give them to? (Open)

5. As you know, the mission of LGLO is to help people physically, educationally, and socially. How do you think we can promote our mission in the community? (Open)

Team Meeting Facilitation

Team meetings, whether they are brainstorming sessions or not, require thought and preparation to make them successful. Team meeting environments involve a host of factors and dynamics that must be managed. To ignore these dynamics can cause difficulties. You don't need to acknowledge all of them verbally, but you need to address them appropriately, either in the meeting or soon after it.

Like the overall workplace, team meetings should have an upbeat tone. They are best conducted with high energy to create positive motivation and momentum. Team meetings will reflect the attitude of the leader, so stay positive even as you highlight areas that need improvement. Instead of criticizing, use team meetings to methodically determine how performance can be improved and to encourage team members toward expectations. Try to facilitate rather than dictate information, and attempt to gain feedback and reinforcement where necessary. When one individual dominates the agenda, people will typically tune out, so assign peer leaders a portion of the agenda. Keep the meeting moving briskly and vary the way content is delivered.

All meetings need to have an agenda, and Rolling Agendas are a great vehicle for facilitating meetings. When rolling agendas are used, the team gets into a rhythm of seeing an agenda with initiatives and actions. At the conclusion of each team meeting, a written summary and list of actions should be created to cover what is to be accomplished and provide the follow-up agenda for the next team meeting.

During team meetings, you can recognize team members' accomplishments, thus reinforcing desired behaviors. Likewise, you can reset expectations and address general areas that need improvement. Avoid singling out poor performers individually in a team meeting because this will detract from your overall message. Save your comments about individual performance improvement for one-on-one meetings. When you mention performance areas where the team needs improvement, typically each person will translate the statement to fit his or her situation without your having to be explicit.

Conclude team meetings by summarizing and reinforcing goals and plans and motivating the team to success. Make sure to leave time for this summary because far too often the clock, not the manager, ends a meeting.

When planning and executing a team meeting, think through the variables to ensure a successful session. You should arrive ten to fifteen minutes prior to the start of the meeting to collect your thoughts and work through any logistics concerning the environment and tools that will be used. This will communicate to the team that you are prepared and will ensure a smooth start to the meeting. A brief checklist of who, where, why, what, when, and how will help. A sample checklist for facilitating meetings appears below.

WHO: PARTICIPANTS
- Who will attend?
- How many participants will there be?
- Which peer leaders and participants will have agenda items?
- What are the strengths of each individual, and what areas should you stay away from?

WHERE: ENVIRONMENT
- Is the meeting in one room or are remote locations involved?
- How should you arrange the room to maximize participation?
- Where should you place presentation aids?

WHY/WHAT/WHEN: ROLLING AGENDA
- Why is the meeting being held?
- What are the goals and plans to be discussed?
- What is the task/action focus?
- When and for how long is each item to be discussed?
- Who will present the item?
- What agenda items will you assign to which peer leaders?

- In what areas do you want newer members of the team to contribute?

HOW: TOOLS AND LOGISTICS
- How will you use your presentation tools (whiteboard, projection equipment, computer, paper handouts, and so on)?
- How will you sequence your agenda to get quick momentum and engagement of the group?
- How will you facilitate discussion?
- How will you use your peer leaders?

Below are abbreviated examples of team meeting facilitation at Acme and LGLO. Notes are provided to illustrate the thought process. The Acme meeting encompasses a principal with thirty teachers, and the LGLO meeting is a manager with three employees, showing both large and small meeting facilitation.

Acme School District Meeting Planning
When planning and facilitating team meetings, you must know exactly what you want to accomplish. It is best to develop the agenda first and then use the checklist to see how it can best be executed. The planning checklist and agenda for the Acme example follow.

PARTICIPANTS
- The principal, 30 teachers, and district coordinators will attend.
- A peer teacher subject-matter expert who uses volunteers effectively and a subject-matter expert in individualized student education will be given speaking assignments.
- The principal will open and close the meeting.
- A district coordinator will be given a speaking assignment on community involvement.

ENVIRONMENT/TOOLS
- Classroom-style seating will be used due to the large number of participants.

- PowerPoint presentations with projection will be used. The principal will arrive 15 minutes early to ready the room and set up computer and presentations.
- Handouts will be placed on desks prior to the start of the meeting: agenda and synopsis.
- Question-and-answer format will be used due to the large group setting.

AGENDA

- The key goal is to review the quarterly progress of district goals and plans.
- The focus will be on community involvement and managing individualized education.
- Presentations will be assigned to one district coordinator and two peer leaders.
- The speakers' presentations will be reviewed before the meeting to make sure they meet the meeting's goals.
- A synopsis of all the speakers' presentations will be developed in a paper format and distributed prior to the meeting so participants can take notes.
- Presentation lengths will be 15 minutes for the principal and teachers and 30 minutes for the district coordinator.
- The sequence of speakers will be principal, district coordinator, peer teachers, and principal.

Acme School District Meeting Execution

The planning checklist results in the following full agenda for the meeting.

Agenda

Goal: Review Quarterly Progress of Goals/Plans

3:00 p.m.–3:15 p.m.: Principal—Review of Goals and Progress
- Student motivation and success
- Academic support

- Learning styles/multimodal instruction
- Community connection

3:15 p.m.–3:45 p.m.: District Coordinator—Community Involvement
- Recruitment of volunteer classroom tutors
- Screening process
- Tutor effectiveness
- Community visits

3:45 p.m.–4:00 p.m.: Peer Teacher—Utilizing Volunteers Effectively
- Managing and delegating to volunteers
- Task specifics
- One-on-one tutoring
- Small group tutoring

4:00 p.m.–4:15 p.m.: Peer Teacher—Lesson Planning/Individualized Student Teaching
- Skill assessments and finding strengths
- Skill mastery and building on skills
- Kinesthetic approaches
- Individualized focus and classroom management

4:15 p.m.–4:30 p.m.: Principal—Meeting Closure
- Summary of key points
- Reinforcement of goals and progress
- Next meeting's schedule and topics

LGLO Specialty Shoe Store Meeting Planning

Here is the same process for a meeting at LGLO. Although this is a much smaller meeting than in the previous example, thorough preparation is nevertheless required.

PARTICIPANTS
- The manager and three employees will attend.
- Peer leaders will discuss 10-step selling process, Medicare, daily specials, and referral program.

- The store manager will open, facilitate, and close the meeting.
- The focus will be on strengths of the peer leaders in an attempt to transfer their behaviors and skills to other employees.

ENVIRONMENT/TOOLS

- A small group setting will be used with four chairs in a circle to maximize interactions and inputs.
- Printed materials to be used are an agenda, goals, plans, and best practices.
- Printed materials will be distributed once participants are seated.
- The manager will facilitate an interactive environment with energy and enthusiasm.
- The two new employees will be asked questions frequently to enhance their understanding of what is expected and to keep them engaged in the meeting.

AGENDA

- The peer leader will be given a speaking assignment.
- The peer leader's materials will be reviewed before the meeting.
- The key goal is to improve execution of goals/plans.
- The focus will be on getting input on plans: customer satisfaction, repeat and referral business, Medicare, and doctor visits.
- A synopsis of the peer leader's presentation will be developed.
- Notes will be taken on all inputs and summarized verbally at the end of the meeting. A written synopsis will be distributed the next day.

LGLO Specialty Shoe Store Meeting Execution

Here is the full agenda for the meeting created using the checklist.

Agenda

Goal: Improvement in Executing Goals/Plans

8:30 a.m.–8:45 a.m.: Store Manager—Review of Goals/Plans

- Customer satisfaction plans
- Risk plans
- Entrepreneurship

8:45 a.m.–9:15 a.m.: Store Manager—Input for Plan Adjustments

- Customer satisfaction surveys: mail, phone
- Repeat business
- Referral business
- Doctor visits

9:15 a.m.–9:45 a.m.: Peer Leader—Best Practices

- 10-step selling process
- Medicare
- Selling daily specials
- Using the referral program

9:45 a.m.–10:00 a.m.: Store Manager—Meeting Closure

- Reinforcement of goals/plans
- Summary of inputs
- Synopsis of peer leader presentation
- Next meeting's schedule and topics

Teamwork

Many managers run their organizations with individual contributors and do not consider teamwork a priority. They prioritize and assess only individual performance. However, achieving results in this manner is more difficult. The sum of the parts is always greater than the individual contributions.

Teamwork in any field is characterized by the principle that at some point, a person in a group is going to have to sacrifice for another.

Sacrifice is important for the greater good of the organization or department and gives the group the ability to more quickly fulfill initiatives. As pointed out previously, successful leaders have sacrificed a tremendous amount in their lives. The more prominent the leaders, the more familiar they are with sacrifice and the need for teamwork.

Teamwork does not just happen. It needs to be intentionally cultivated and developed. A team orientation ought to be exhibited by all leaders and must be modeled consistently by the manager. Unless the team's focus is pointed to the organization's mission, vision, culture, goals, and plans, fragmentation will occur. Good teams support members individually and hold each other accountable through peer leadership with a minimum amount of managerial intercession. It is up to you to create the environment, set the example, and consistently nurture teamwork.

You can create a team environment in a number of ways. For example, all organizations benefit when team members share best practices and explain how they specifically apply their knowledge and skills. You need to provide a forum at meetings, training sessions, lunches, social events, and so on, to foster sharing and in turn facilitate team bonding and unity.

Identify areas that need improvement within the team and facilitate training and skill development sessions to address them. Ask team members with strengths in these areas to share best practices. Best practice sharing is great for both knowledge transfer and motivation.

As managers, we have access to a plethora of human resources that we can use to fulfill a mission and goals. Regardless of our intellect and experience levels, none of us have the ability to accomplish great goals by ourselves. We need to realize our own weaknesses and supplement them with other people's strengths.

When you do this yourself and delegate effectively, a team will emerge that can exceed all individual expectations. All people have a need to feel the sense of significance they get when they contribute to something greater than themselves, and your role is to develop the team philosophy to fulfill this need.

Quick Reference

Because people tend to be individualistic, it can be difficult to teach them to achieve common goals, but a team atmosphere is vital because people working together will always yield greater results than individuals working alone. The foundational tenet of teamwork is that at some point, an individual will have to sacrifice something for the good of the group. This chapter examined ways to develop good teamwork with a positive team environment, consistent rhythm, effective brainstorming, and better team meetings.

Environment

- If you consistently make decisions in the best interest of the group, you model teamwork that becomes a standard mode of operation.

- Positive energy is created when activity levels are high and tasks are being accomplished by all group members.

- When you create positive momentum, people want to contribute.

- All team members must feel like they are contributing or discord can occur.

Rhythm

- Consistency in meetings and schedules establishes a healthy rhythm and facilitates a team focus.

- In addition to measuring short-term progress, you can use weekly meetings to frame and reinforce the organizational mission and goals.

- You must avoid canceling weekly meetings or a healthy rhythm can be lost. Any schedule changes must be communicated to team members as far in advance as possible.

- In addition to team meetings, short sessions should be scheduled with individuals early in the week to get insight into their motivation, objectives, and priorities.

Questions and Brainstorming Techniques

- Good questioning techniques will uncover creative ideas and facilitate learning in those you manage.
- To facilitate brainstorming sessions, you can write the goals, problems, or initiatives to be addressed for all to view.
- You need to be diligent in suppressing negativity during the brainstorming sessions or it can quickly get out of control.
- Good brainstorming sessions bond team members and create momentum for the ultimate plan or solution when it is launched.
- You can start each brainstorming session by presenting a list of ideas you have formulated so as to initiate feedback.
- You need to make it clear that all ideas are welcome but will not necessarily be implemented.
- You must insist on a positive environment free from criticism and negativity.
- It's helpful to conclude with a summary of ideas, referring to ideas from each team member who participated.

Team Meeting Facilitation

- Team meetings require thought and preparation to make them successful. Rolling agendas can help.
- You need to stay positive because your attitude will set the tone of team meetings.
- You should keep the meetings moving briskly and vary the way content is delivered by assigning a portion of the agenda to peer leaders.
- You can use team meetings to recognize accomplishments, but poor performers should not be singled out.

Teamwork

- Fostering teamwork is your responsibility, so you need to consistently model team orientation.

- Good teams support members individually and hold each other accountable with a minimum amount of managerial intercession.
- You need to provide opportunities for team members to share best practices.
- When you delegate effectively, a team will emerge that can exceed all individual expectations.

CHAPTER 7

Honing Your Interpersonal Management Skills

A LONG WITH TACTICAL and team development skills, all managers must continuously hone their interpersonal management skills. Regardless of your organizational position, management is about people and your ability to relate to them and motivate them. Good interpersonal management skills are essential in driving a team to fulfill the organization's mission and goals.

This chapter closely parallels many of the topics covered in part 1 of the book. It is intended to reinforce key areas and discuss them in a specific management context.

Personal Management Philosophies

Before you are able to manage effectively, the members of your team must know what to expect. Establishing a baseline for interactions lets team members know exactly where you stand on expectations, issues, and behaviors. This need is best addressed when you develop a personal management philosophies document to share with them.

The personal management philosophies document sets guidelines for interactions and problem resolution. It provides a reference point for interviewing and a reference document for team member management.

You are not attempting to force your philosophies upon a candidate or subordinate; rather, you are communicating clear guidelines of how you will operate.

The personal management philosophies document reflects your fundamental beliefs about management and lets people know what you expect. Share this document with all candidates who want to be a part of your team or organization and use it to compare philosophies with the individuals you manage or recruit. For example, if you strive to engender teamwork and prefer a team concept and you interview someone who expresses a preference to work independently, you have identified a difference in approach. The management philosophies document enables you to address a mismatch in the early stages of your interaction with a person, determine if a role on your team is a fit for that individual, and avoid potential issues and difficulties in the future.

The management philosophies document should reflect who you are as a manager and a person. To create it, you will need to think carefully and determine your philosophy and style. Put your management philosophies into a written document that does not exceed one page. Give each member of your team a copy, and then refer to pertinent items in the document as situations arise in the day-to-day routine. For example, suppose one of your management philosophies is "Insist on thorough preparation from everyone in all activities." If the team needs to prepare for an upcoming task or someone comes to a meeting unprepared, you can remind people that thorough preparation is what you expect. You will probably find that you need to refine specific areas in your management philosophies document to become more effective.

Management Philosophy Examples

The following two examples illustrate personal management philosophies documents for a principal in the Acme School District and the store manager at LGLO Specialty Shoe Store.

Management Philosophies: Greg Klass, Acme School District Principal

- Always make decisions in the best interests of the students and school district, not myself.

- Work in unison with all stakeholders to accomplish the school district's mission.
- Develop a one-to-one partnership with each teacher to build, develop and manage effectively.
- Leverage the one-to-one partnerships to build on strengths and improve weaker areas.
- Supplement the individual's improvement-needed areas with training and development opportunities.
- Emphasize communication and communication skills.
- Insist on thorough preparation from everyone in all activities.
- Communicate expectations repeatedly and regularly.
- Adjust/reprioritize quickly when required.
- Force conflict resolution to the lowest common denominator.
- Use humor to help people feel good and enjoy what they are doing.
- Test and assess students frequently to make sure they demonstrate foundational skill mastery and no student falls behind.
- Forge a personal connection to the community.
- Apply original thinking and creativity to the job.
- Show a good example by accomplishing administrative tasks before deadlines.

Management Philosophies: Karen Wrangler, LGLO Specialty Shoe Store Manager

- Always do what is best for the customer.
- Team with owners and subordinates to jointly accomplish the organization's mission and goals.
- Apply the organization's mission and goals to the details in each task.
- Focus on performance, not the person, when improvement is required.
- Encourage customers and employees at all times.
- Focus on people management verses numbers management.

- Provide team-building opportunities in meetings, training sessions, lunches, and elsewhere.
- Quantify performance based on expectations.
- Provide regular feedback on each employee's performance as spelled out in the employee's job description and expectations.
- Implement and manage a defined process to achieve goals.
- Address potential issues and conflicts proactively so they don't escalate.
- Manage the organization as if I own it.
- Never allow myself or any employees to say "That's not my job."
- Always exhibit an empathetic character when interacting with customers.
- Constantly evaluate the overall effectiveness of personnel, systems, and processes.

As you may have noticed, Greg's document has several parallels to the school district's goals. His philosophy of working in unison with stakeholders closely aligns with Acme's goal of connecting students to the community. His belief in leveraging partnerships is similar to Acme's goal of providing students academic support in a variety of ways. His philosophy of testing and assessing students frequently perfectly fits Acme's goal of assessing students to make sure they have mastered a foundational academic skill before moving to the next. In fact, each of these management philosophies in Greg's document shows a close connection to Acme's mission. These similarities are a way to explore and potentially predict a good fit for Greg and Acme.

Likewise, Karen's management philosophies have similarities to LGLO's mission and goals. Her first belief, "Always do what is best for the customer," is the number one goal of LGLO. The fact that Karen put this so high on her list is a good sign of compatibility. Her philosophy of providing team-building opportunities is very much like LGLO's goal of creating a store environment emphasizing motivation and teamwork. Her belief in exhibiting an empathetic character when interacting with customers is much the same as LGLO's mission of helping people physically, educationally, and socially. As with Greg and Acme, you can see how Karen's management philosophies are very similar to LGLO's mission and goals and provide a great foundation of discussion for both parties.

Consultative Approach

One key item in any manager's philosophy should be to always position oneself as a resource and consultant to team members. The authoritative or dictatorial approach usually doesn't yield good results. The consultative approach, on the other hand, emphasizes that you put others first. Using this approach, managers coach team members to help them achieve their professional and personal goals as long as achievement of these goals is in line with organizational goals and is not at the expense of others.

When you take a consultative approach, you use your experience, knowledge and wisdom to advance the skills of your team members. This mentorship will provide great satisfaction for both you and your team members. In taking a consultative approach and putting the team members' needs first, you show sacrifice, which helps establish trust, respect, and teamwork. You show that you value the individuals who work for you and build an interpersonal bridge to partnership while maintaining the necessary chain of command in the organizational structure.

To offer coaching, mentoring, and advice that are of value to individuals, you need an insatiable appetite for learning your particular craft or field. There is no excuse for managers not to be motivated to learn and better themselves. With the rapid acceleration of technology, knowledge acquisition is made easier all the time. As you research and learn, you will become more and more of a resource in your field and to the people you manage.

The consultative approach should become part of your mind-set and extend beyond the people you manage to their larger networks. Those within and outside your organization are great sources of knowledge. It's easy to become myopic if you are focused only on your own organization. In addition, managers who can share their experiences outside their organizations can be viewed as trusted advisors in their fields.

The consultative approach is best framed in a humble manner. An arrogant or condescending approach quickly turns people off. Nobody likes a braggart, and even a good message delivered improperly will be compromised. The basis of the consultative approach is to share with, consult with, and help other people who in turn help you and the organization.

Relationship to Partnership

Another key interpersonal management skill is the ability to build on individual relationships and help them progress to valuable and productive partnerships. We know that people work better when they connect with one another and get along. We have also seen that the leader is responsible for creating an environment that facilitates both group and individual relationships. Strong partnerships enable managers to work with team members with minimal resistance and maximum buy-in.

Try to build rapport with every individual you manage. When you are interacting with people who have similar personalities, rapport building is a relatively easy task. It is more difficult to create rapport and engender relationships with those who don't have a lot in common with you. Regardless of commonalities or personality compatibilities, you must develop relationships with all team members to produce trust because without mutual trust, it is difficult to form partnerships.

Good relationships naturally grow into partnerships to achieve common goals. When mutual trust and partnerships are established, team members can flourish. The team becomes more effective and productive. Not only are an organization's goals accomplished, but all people involved in their pursuit experience more satisfaction and have more fun.

To establish individual partnerships, you need to begin by assigning tasks that can be readily accomplished. Achieving tasks nurtures mutual satisfaction and creates momentum toward fulfilling larger organizational objectives. As individuals execute their duties, you can assign more complex responsibilities to stretch them and accomplish more valuable goals for the organization. As the partnerships grow, you can delegate more tasks and accomplish more in your own role. In turn the team members can grow and become more aware of their areas of strength and weakness. Once these areas are apparent, you will have a much easier time mapping training and development plans for the team members.

To turn relationships into partnerships, you need to come alongside individual team members with the express intent of helping them develop to their full potential. Through words and actions, you must communicate that there is joint ownership of their success.

Additionally, you have to be aware of team members' personal needs because these frequently affect their motivation. It is a delicate balance to be aware of people's personal needs without becoming overly involved in their personal lives. You have to encourage people according to their needs, both personally and professionally, while maintaining a degree of separation so that you can continue to be effective and objective in your role as a manager.

Management Separation

One of the most difficult disciplines managers must master is having the necessary degree of separation from the people they oversee. A common mistake new managers can make (and also a trap for experienced managers) is becoming overly friendly with the individuals they supervise. This is not to say that friendships can't exist, but managers have to constantly monitor their interpersonal relationships to make sure they keep an arm's length between themselves and their team members.

If managers become overly friendly with a single person or multiple people, they risk losing trust and credibility with their team. Whether it's true or not, team members will feel they are not being treated fairly and equitably.

Without separation, your leadership and character can be called into question. For example, you need to have separation to discuss job performance effectively; any appearance of favoritism can quickly torpedo your credibility. Management separation necessitates that all decisions be made in a professional and objective manner, regardless of your relationship with an individual.

Conflict Resolution

Another interpersonal management skill is the ability to handle conflict. Conflict can arise in virtually any situation, and you must anticipate it. It can occur with people at any level in the organizational hierarchy. As long as two or more people are gathered, they will have varying opinions and may disagree.

You need to be aware of situations or attitudes that could lead to conflict and address them before they escalate. This requires being keenly aware of the circumstances and pressure that can cause potential conflicts. Conflict resolution is a difficult discipline to learn because most of us do not like conflict or confrontation. The simplest but least effective choice is to avoid addressing potential conflicts and hope they go away. This approach leads to festering disputes, and disruptions can occur because the manager did not have the discipline or emotional strength to address the situation as it was unfolding.

Be aware of the individual personal and motivational needs of your team members and how they can impact the organizational environment. If you can address challenges before they become big issues, you can avoid big conflicts. Awareness is a leadership skill that can help. You must develop awareness to see more in depth and farther than others. You must also be aware of patterns and anticipate conflicts before they occur. Be aware of the big picture, stay on an even keel, and resolve conflicts in the best interests of the organization.

Being a manager means being prepared emotionally and psychologically for potential conflict at all times. Some say that managers need to intervene in situations as a form of "care-frontation." This means that managers try to defuse situations with care and empathy and not anger and frustration. Because calm in the face of adversity is the sign of a great leader, your calmness and proficiency in dealing with challenges and difficult situations will bring you respect.

Addressing conflicts requires different tactics based on the severity of the conflict. Minor conflicts can be resolved quickly with a minimum of strategic thought. Major conflicts will take more thought and time to resolve. Whether the conflict is between you and a subordinate or between two subordinates, you should be consistent in getting input to bring forth a resolution. When faced with a major decision, gather all pertinent information before acting. Seek input with closed questioning techniques because conflict resolution requires that you have a firm hand and be responsible for the final decision.

All techniques to resolve conflicts should be methodical and unemotional in nature. Sometimes the best way to defuse a situation is to exaggerate the circumstances so much and make the potential ramifications so big that the people in conflict can see the ridiculousness of the situation and see the lack of thought or maturity on their parts. Then a resolution can come quickly. This technique is best used for minor situations.

Let's use an example from LGLO Specialty Shoe Store. One of LGLO's goals is to maintain a positive store environment through furniture placement and refreshments. Karen, the manager, delegates this task to store employees Joe and Chad. Joe and Chad have an ongoing minor conflict over where to place the furniture and what type of juice to serve the customers. Karen determines that she has to address the conflict before it escalates. Because it is a minor conflict, she chooses to exaggerate the situation in hopes that Joe and Chad will realize how immature the squabble really is.

Karen calls a meeting with Joe and Chad and says she doesn't appreciate their inability to resolve their issues over the furniture placement and juice selection. She asks them if the difference between serving apple juice and orange juice is really going to make a difference in sales. Will the juice being served adversely affect their families, the city, or the country? She asks if the juice or where a table is placed is a big enough issue for them to get upset about. Once Karen sees that the employees have realized how petty the issue really is, she suggests they talk about it and come up with their own resolution. She suggests that they may want to alternate the furniture placement and juices each day but leaves the ultimate resolution up to them.

Typically, the best way to defuse major or highly charged emotional situations is to minimize the circumstances objectively, seek inputs, and offer two or three alternative solutions that may resolve the conflict. You have to do this by defusing emotions and realistically looking at the severity of the conflict. Once the situation is in perspective, the best course of action can be decided upon and communicated to the combatants.

To best illustrate this technique, we will use an example from the Acme School District. In the district's goal of providing a comprehensive academic support structure, a major conflict has arisen between the district training coordinator and a classroom teacher. The coordinator has been tasked with implementing a screening and training program for classroom tutors that adheres to district guidelines. The teacher is bypassing the guidelines and using her own tutors, who have not been screened. She is using friends and acquaintances as tutors, so she has a personal emotional attachment to them. Rumors have circulated that one of the tutors may have had some legal issues in the past. The superintendent of the Acme School District has asked Principal Greg to resolve this issue as soon as possible.

Greg realizes the seriousness of the issue and the emotions in play. He convenes a meeting and handles it in the following manner: "Thank you both for coming on such short notice. As you both know, we have a serious issue that needs to get resolved. The superintendent has asked me to resolve this quickly, and I ask that you help me do it. As you know, we have a firm commitment to providing academic support for our students and use a variety of methods to accomplish it. We also have district policies to adhere to. I know that you both are committed to our students."

To the coordinator Greg says, "I know you are doing a good job implementing our district policy. We need to make sure that our district people are aware of all the challenges our classroom teachers face and act accordingly."

To the teacher Greg says, "I know that you are a good teacher and really love your students. We need to make sure our school employees realize the responsibilities of our district people and make sure we work together to accomplish the Acme mission."

Greg then speaks in a firm manner to both the coordinator and the teacher: "You both know we are dealing with a conflict between you in regard to our academic support structure and tutors. I know you both think what you are doing is right, but we have to make some immediate adjustments. A perception exists that we are allowing unscreened tutors to interact with our students, which is not in adherence to district policy. I know that there are a lot of reasons for this, but frankly, I think you are both contributing to this conflict and are potentially putting our district and students at risk. I don't think either of you intended to do this, but that is where the situation stands."

Greg then communicates the resolution. Because this conflict is of a serious nature with far-reaching implications, he does not solicit input from either the coordinator or the teacher. "I would ask that both of you immediately adhere to district policy on this matter." To the coordinator he says, "I would ask that there be no further delays in screening the candidates put forth by this teacher." To the teacher he says, "I would ask that anyone who desires to be in contact with our students as a tutor be screened immediately in line with our district guidelines."

Speaking to both parties, he says, "We will meet in one week to discuss progress and specifics on this resolution. Is the plan clear to you both?" At this point, Greg must get verbal confirmation from both parties before moving on. "Thank you again for meeting with me on short notice. I would also suggest you meet with each other to better understand each other's concerns. We want to make sure that you have a professional working relationship moving forward and that we try to avoid this type of conflict in the future. Sound good?" Greg also has to make sure he gets confirmation from both parties after this statement.

Too many managers get roped into being the judge in the disputes of two subordinates. Instead, you should first frame the dispute in objective terms and then ask the two participants to attempt to resolve the issue themselves. The resolution they present may not be the one that you would provide, but the main goal is for the participants to confront each other, sit down and talk about the issue, and come to a resolution. Not only is the problem resolved in this way, but you have created an environment and relational pattern by which the department or organization can handle future conflicts. Conflict should be resolved on the lowest possible level of the organization, preferably by the people involved with minimal management intervention.

For example, two teachers in the Acme School District are in a dispute regarding field trips. One teacher thinks the students should be visiting more museums, while the other thinks they should visit more businesses. Each teacher has come to Principal Greg, sharing her opinion.

Greg reviews the situation and realizes it is not a big issue. A trip to either a museum or a business meets the district goal, and Greg wants to make sure these two teachers can resolve these types of disputes without him in the future.

He convenes a meeting with both teachers. He first tells the teachers he is extremely pleased that they both are striving hard to accomplish the district's goal of community connection. He tells them that he has reviewed the previous field trip visits and is happy with the results. He then relates that both of them have contacted him individually about their opinions on the next field trips. Greg says that because both their ideas meet the stated goal, he sees no problem with either one. He then tells them that he really wants to establish an environment where teachers can resolve relatively minor conflicts with minimum intervention on his part. He suggests the teachers meet one-on-one to come up with a resolution. Greg then sets a meeting in one week's time to hear their resolution.

Conflict resolutions between a manager and a subordinate should exhibit a completely different tone of conversation than peer-to-peer resolutions. You always need to put forth tangible ideas and see if the conflict can be resolved in that manner. The best-case scenario is where the conflict falls within outlined ideas in your management philosophies, job descriptions, or expectations. By referring to these documents, you can frame the discussion in such a way as to remove emotions and address the situation objectively and specifically.

The process needs to be unemotional and not argumentative. Prepare yourself by studying the expectations document for the subordinate. (You'll learn how to create an expectations document in part 3.) Make notes as to what you are going to say so the conversation does not get off course. Stay specific and on topic in the discussion.

Be sure to note other areas where the subordinate is doing a good job before and after you discuss the area of conflict. Before you conclude the meeting, ask the subordinate if he or she understands what you expect. Follow up with a short note summarizing what was discussed. Again, frame the note with the many things the subordinate is doing right and ask for compliance in the one area of conflict that needs improvement.

Conflict is one of the most difficult situations you must handle, and it can have huge ramifications on team members' motivation, credibility, and mutual trust. You must therefore put into practice a framework by which disputes can be resolved and stay consistent with the process.

Performance Coaching

Performance coaching is used to develop and motivate an individual or team to execute to the highest level. Coaching sessions are done in both team and one-on-one meetings. We discussed team coaching in the section on team meeting facilitation (chapter 6) and will focus on one-on-one performance coaching in this section.

One-on-one coaching affords you the opportunity to discuss an individual's personal and professional goals. You and the team member can advance your relationship and better develop your partnership.

The session should be both open ended and specific. You can start by asking open-ended questions such as "How is it going?" and "How do you like your role?" The specific discussion should be guided by performance expectations, job descriptions, and organizational goals.

Effective performance coaching necessitates a consultative approach. You need to be willing to go as far as offering career counseling if necessary. Try to understand the individual's personal goals, long-term plans, and vision and to convey a genuine interest in the individual's story, and his or her development. This is a good time to gauge how much trust to put in the team member and, likewise, how much trust the team member has in you.

The goal of the one-on-one performance coaching discussion is to agree on strengths, areas of needed improvement, and the unique value the individual brings to the organization. The value discussion should center on two areas: personal and professional. Personal value emphasizes general skills such as communication, integrity, and perseverance. Professional value is related to role-specific areas such as knowledge in the field, personal and professional networks, expectation fulfillment, and so on. In both cases, you set a tremendous example when you come alongside and help individuals in their personal and professional development because it shows you value them and want to help them fulfill their potential.

Performance coaching sessions should take place at least monthly. To structure the meeting, fill out a performance expectations document and take time to analyze it to ensure accuracy. If significant performance improvement is required, you should meet with the individual weekly. In these sessions, you and the team member should codevelop strategies and plans for improvement with mutually agreed-upon objectives that are measurable and relate specifically to the performance expectations.

When significant performance improvement in a particular area is required, address the issue immediately. For example, Joyce, the superintendent of the Acme School District, is coaching Greg, a principal. She has determined that Greg is exceeding expectations in most areas. However, he needs substantial improvement in three areas listed in the

Acme monthly expectations document for school site principals (see pages 140–142). Joyce will meet with Greg weekly to help coach him in the performance areas in which he does not meet expectations.

Joyce uses the expectations document and frames the discussion in the following manner: "Greg, overall we think you are doing a great job as a principal in the Acme School District. You have adopted the mission and are doing well in achieving our district goals. The school is doing well relative to learning style testing, lesson plan compliance with state standards, and technology utilization. We are struggling in a few areas, and I would like to work closely with you in improving them. The areas are state standard content instruction, multimodal lesson planning, and multimodal instruction. As you know, those initiatives are very important to achieving our district goals. How do you think we are doing in those areas?"

In this way, Joyce has laid the framework for the three areas of improvement and can now discuss them one by one with Greg. She can ask what he thinks, what suggestions he has for improvement, what plans can be enacted, and what specific actions they can take by next week. Should the session steer off course, Joyce can refer back to the expectations document to get it back on track. From this meeting, a plan should surface, developed by Greg and used as a weekly agenda. This plan will relate directly to the expectations areas that need improvement.

During a performance coaching session, focus on the way you verbally deliver feedback as much as the content to ensure that productive communication is taking place. Remember to focus on the performance, not the person, when you communicate strengths and areas that need improvement. The words "feedback," "review," and "performance discussion" can make us all nervous because we associate them with negative experiences. When addressing performance areas to be improved, never say "You need to improve" but rather "This area of performance needs to improve." If people receiving coaching take something personally, they tend to stop paying attention and the rest of the session is lost.

The personal part of the session is intended to develop a partnership. The professional part of the session focuses on expectations, and you should conduct it in a nonemotional manner.

During these sessions set high expectations and measure against them to stretch the performance of your team members. If you consistently communicate high expectations and accountability in team meetings and one-on-one coaching sessions, you will not have to constantly apply pressure. The high expectations will become part of the daily routine and culture.

Don't allow the discussion to revolve around obstacles. It needs to be a "make it happen" session. The "Will and Focus" section in chapter 2 covers several ideas that apply to high-expectation setting in coaching sessions. Will is the ability to project success before a task is undertaken. You must set the tone by expressing without hesitation or doubt that an initiative will be realized. Keep team members focused on major initiatives as well as their individual expectations so the mission and goals of the organization can be fulfilled.

Performance coaching discussions can easily become derailed or tangential, so you need to keep them on track or they will be a waste of time for both participants. Use the performance expectations as the basis of the conversation. Apply the sandwich principle when giving coaching feedback, and make sure the individual leaves the session with positive motivation and encouragement.

Inevitably, you will sometimes decide that an individual is not the right fit for a certain role or for the organization. You should determine this after several performance coaching sessions, consultation with others in the management hierarchy, and in-depth assessment. When a decision is being made about parting ways, you should plant the seeds of potential separation from the organization in coaching sessions. Do this early in the process if you've seen multiple warning signs that the role is not a fit. Directly ask the individual if he or she thinks the role or organization is a long-term fit based on the person's job description and expectations. If this conversation is had in the right manner, the individual should be able to see the issues and may seek alternatives. Emphasize that you want the individual to be successful, even if it is not in his or her current role or with the current organization. Spend some time trying to find a role inside or outside your organization where the individual can have a soft landing and be successful in the future. Experienced managers realize that if an individual needs to leave a role or organization, both parties have failed in some way.

Performance coaching sessions are critical whether a person is exceeding expectations or has to be managed out of the organization.

To make these sessions more effective, be sure to set an example with your own job description and expectations. You are constantly being watched and critiqued. If you are not setting an example for all the desired behaviors you have communicated to your team, your team members will think you are hypocritical. Note that you are held to higher standards than those you manage. Setting an example is the most effective way to coach and teach.

Coaching by pointing out a mistake, promoting learning from it, and enabling a person to sustain motivation in the process is an art. You must develop the ability to consistently, honestly, and objectively assess your own strengths and areas of needed improvement as well as to have meaningful discussions with team members. Bring your own strengths and development areas into the discussion so the conversation is not one sided. Assess whether or not you have been approachable, whether you have an open-door policy, and whether your attitude and conversation reflect the requisite leadership necessary to motivate someone. All these factors contribute to realistic and effective performance coaching sessions.

Networking

People are the best sources of knowledge in any endeavor. An expanded network of people enables you to draw from a large pool of knowledgeable sources for counsel and for recruitment. Good managers intentionally schedule time in their calendars weekly to reach out and broaden their network of people.

Developing a large network enables you to know what is going on beyond your own organization and outside your field. Should you get too myopically focused on your organization, you cannot keep up with best practices and trends or stay in touch with helpful people. Another huge benefit of networking is that it enables you to become a valuable personal and professional resource to others. If you are viewed as a good resource of knowledge and contacts, people will seek you out on a variety of topics, and new opportunities will surface.

Having a large network will also enable you to more easily and quickly lay a broad information base for your organization's goals and plans. All the people in your organization need to get the word out on what the organization is and what it does. In fact, they are the best and most credible advertising you have. When you enlarge the organization's contact base and team members tell everyone they meet about the organization, opportunities will abound. Developing and enlarging your network of people is not only fun but very profitable as well.

Change and Transition

The last interpersonal management skill to be discussed in this chapter is managing change and transition. It is said that the only thing in life that is constant is change. Most human beings resist change, and many don't cope well with it. Good managers anticipate change and see it as an opportunity to improve. They do not shy away from challenges but embrace them. They ask how a challenge can make their organization better and how it will help develop their own character. Apply this same attitude to change and embrace it as a situation that can benefit you.

Similar to change are the challenges that come with transition. We all would like to have an extremely stable personnel environment from which to build initiatives and continuity, but organizations are much more transient than they were in the past.

Transitions are a fact of life, and good managers have to anticipate them and plan for them. Like change, transitions are an opportunity to think strategically and determine how you and your organization can improve. If you continually perceive change and transition as negatives, you will cause yourself undue stress. Rather, look at them as constant variables, opportunities, and challenges that you factor into the big picture and that move your department or organization closer to key goals.

Quick Reference

Regardless of your position in the organization, management is about people and your ability to relate to them and motivate them. This chapter took many of the concepts from part 1 and looked at them in the context of day-to-day management.

Personal Management Philosophies

- The personal management philosophies document establishes exactly where you stand on expectations, issues, and behaviors and sets guidelines for interactions and problem resolution.

- It provides a reference point for interviewing so you can identify a mismatch early and determine whether a candidate is a good fit for a particular role.
- You can use your management philosophies document in conflict resolution to remove emotions and address the situation objectively.

Consultative Approach

- The basis of the consultative approach is to share with, consult with, and help other people so you can achieve initiatives for your organization.
- You can use your experience, knowledge, and wisdom to advance the skills of your team members.
- When you take a consultative approach and put the team members' needs first, you show sacrifice, which helps establish trust, respect, and teamwork.
- When you share your experiences outside the organization, you will be viewed as a trusted advisor in your field.

Relationship to Partnership

- Regardless of personality compatibilities, you must develop good relationships with all team members to produce trust.
- The natural outgrowth of a good relationship is that it becomes a partnership to achieve common goals.
- As the partnership grows, you will be able to delegate more tasks and in turn accomplish more in your own role as manager.

Management Separation

- If your relationship with one or more team members becomes overly friendly, you risk losing trust and credibility with your team.
- When difficult circumstances or situations arise, a perception of favoritism can result.
- Without separation, your leadership and character will be called into question.

- You must make decisions in a professional and objective manner, regardless of your relationship with an individual.

Conflict Resolution

- Your role as a manager requires you to be prepared emotionally and psychologically for potential conflicts at all times.
- If you can anticipate and address challenges before they escalate, you can avoid big conflicts.
- Conflicts should be resolved at the lowest possible level of the organization with minimal management intervention.
- You must put into practice a framework by which disputes can be resolved and stay consistent with the process.

Performance Coaching

- The goal of performance coaching is to agree on strengths, areas of needed improvement, and the unique value the individual brings to the organization.
- Performance expectations should form the basis of the conversation.
- You need to focus on the performance, not the person.
- If you don't keep performance coaching discussions on track, they can easily become a waste of time for both participants.

Networking

- Having a large network of people helps you know what is going on in your community and field.
- You should schedule time in your calendar weekly to reach out and broaden your network of people.
- If you are viewed as a good resource, people will seek you out on a variety of topics.
- You should strive to enlarge your contact base and tell everyone you meet about the organization.

Change and Transition

- You must look at change and transition as opportunities to move your department or organization closer to key goals.

- Changes and transitions are facts of life, and a good manager has to anticipate and plan for them.

- If you continually perceive change and transition as negatives, you will cause yourself undue stress.

PART III

Administration

T HIS PART OF the book offers practical administrative tools and examples that will help you apply the ideas from part 2. Leaders must execute plans so team members can see the organizational mission, vision, and goals in the details of their administrative work. Otherwise, they will approach administrative tasks in a mundane manner, which will lead to a less-than-optimum quality of work.

The examples in this section illustrate how to apply key management principles to administrative tasks. The management topics in part 3 include job descriptions and expectations, recruiting and interviewing, hiring and orientation, and an organization's information base. You'll also learn about key administrative skills, including time management, calendar setting, note taking, and presentations.

CHAPTER 8

Applying Administrative Tools and Techniques

A S W E H A V E seen, people are your most important resource. This chapter shows how to help the people on your team be successful, how to find new people for your team, and how to spread the word about the organization to people outside it.

The key to helping people succeed in their roles is a job description document that clearly spells out what you expect and gives you an objective way to discuss team members' performance. This document will also help when it's time to recruit new people to the organization. Strategies in this chapter include how to use your network to find the best people and how to handle the interview process so that you bring on winners, not just survivors.

Just as you need to take a calculated approach to interviewing and recruiting, you must also prepare thoroughly for the entrance of new people to your organization. Your number one responsibility in the first couple of weeks is to get new people settled into their roles, help them gain confidence, and set them up for success.

This chapter also explains the role of an information base in achieving an organization's mission. You will learn how to create an information base so that everyone is presenting the same message about the organization. As a result, people in the community will begin to understand what sets your organization apart and new opportunities will surface.

Job Descriptions and Expectations

People are much more comfortable executing what is expected if their roles are clearly defined. Therefore, you need to make sure individual team members know their roles and tasks specifically and in detail. All too often team members are confused about expectations and priorities, which can lead them to "make it up as they go" or simply do what they used to do in a previous job. Clear job descriptions and expectations prevent this behavior.

Job descriptions and expectations need to be communicated and reinforced in both written and verbal ways. A job description should be a concise synopsis of what is required of an individual in a specific role. Expectations should expand on the job description and provide specific details that equate to success in the role.

A job description should clearly state the function a person is to perform. Too often job descriptions are compromised as organizations try to fill holes with one particular person and roles become diluted and blurry. An organization can get off track easily if individuals do not follow job descriptions. Best practice dictates that job descriptions be a natural extension of organizational goals, plans, and expected tasks. Good job descriptions reflect the natural flow from mission to goals to plans to tasks and clearly link the tasks to the accomplishment of the mission.

Once you have created specific job descriptions, you can develop expectation documents to measure performance against the job descriptions. Refer to these expectations consistently and conduct formal reviews monthly, quarterly, and annually. Consistent reviews demand a tremendous amount of discipline on your part because this administrative task can be time-consuming. However, expectation reviews are the only way to link back to the job description and give individuals truly objective insight into their performance.

Job descriptions and expectations should not be filed away but rather referred to when conducting monthly, quarterly, and annual performance reviews. Clearly stated expectations minimize subjectivity in the feedback process and enable you to give forward direction to those you guide.

Expectation documents need specific metrics and key performance parameters so you can address them with subordinates in feedback sessions. You can then link the individual expectations to key goals and show how they correlate to overall organizational objectives.

When you communicate feedback about expectations, focus on the person receiving it. Referring to numbers and data is beneficial, but you must relate them to the performance of the person in front of you. Your role is to coach the individual to meet expectations.

As you deliver expectation coaching, monitor the emotional reception of the individual receiving the feedback. If you are too harsh or personal when discussing the areas of needed improvement, the person may check out mentally, and the rest of the meeting can be a waste of time. Remember the sandwich principle: start the communication with something positive, communicate the performance area that needs improvement as specifically and measurably as possible, and then end with a positive comment, making sure you gain agreement on both the area of improvement and the areas of strength.

Following are examples of job descriptions and expectations for Acme and LGLO. They are intended to show how job descriptions and expectations are built from the mission, goals, and plans of an organization.

These examples are in narrative form, but feel free to provide expectations in any format, including spreadsheet, narrative, and so on. Some positions may require a scoring system, but try to stay away from that if possible. When you give feedback to team members using a scoring system, oftentimes they may focus too much on the numbers and miss the substance of what you are trying to communicate. This makes for a poor expectations discussion.

Job Description for Acme School District

The following job description was created by the Acme School District to specifically describe the job of principal in the district.

Title: School Site Principal
Location: San Diego, CA
Type: Salaried Full Time

School District Description
The Acme School District is a progressive district that applies educational concepts to individual students and provides opportunities for them to connect to their communities. Acme's charter is to develop its students into lifelong learners who progress in their own learning styles and are involved in their local communities. The Acme School District is widely recognized as a beacon for applying creative methodologies to teach and develop its students and staff. Its personnel are recognized as the best and brightest in the field of education.

General Summary
The school site principal is a leader who applies Acme's mission, goals, and plans in a practical way on campus and in the community. The principal must nurture an environment in which students, teachers, and support staff personally own the district's vision and are motivated to ensure students enjoy learning and have individual success. The principal role requires excellent leadership skills and experience in managing diverse groups of people. Excellent interpersonal and communication skills are a must.

Essential Duties and Responsibilities
- Create, nurture, and maintain an environment in which students are motivated, achieve individual success, and enjoy learning.
- Align individual student strengths and interests to instruction that shows relevance and increases student motivation.
- Manage teaching and administrative support staff to attain the Acme School District mission and goals.
- Provide an academic support system that enables students to succeed to the best of their abilities.
- Recruit, organize, and manage nondistrict personnel to increase overall resources to help achieve the Acme School District mission.
- Manage teaching staff to fulfill the goal of measuring each student's academic progress on a monthly basis.
- Ensure diverse methodologies are being used in each classroom to stimulate individual students' best learning style.

- Manage continuity and consistency of classroom instruction to align to state standard content.
- Develop innovative programs utilizing technology to reinforce instructional content.
- Be a visible and involved part of the local community
- Provide students the opportunity to become part of the community through hands-on involvement and experiences.

Required Experience
- Minimum of five years of educational administrative experience
- Documented high performance in the field of education
- Management and financial background preferred

Required Education
- BA Administrative Education
- MA Administrative Education preferred

Acme School Site Principal Monthly Expectations

The following monthly expectations document is based on the job description for principals. It expands on the job description and provides specific details that equate to success in the role.

The two columns provide a format for execution and evaluation. The first expected column contains the four key goals of the Acme School District, along with a fifth area to evaluate overall administrative performance. The tasks under each goal are the steps required to achieve that goal. It is important to place all your key expectations in this column. As you can see, the essential duties and responsibilities in the job description are broken down into specific actionable tasks in the expectations document.

The second column offers space to evaluate how the person is doing compared to the expectations. It is used to provide an objective, concise analysis of the individual's performance regarding the organization's key goals and plans.

Name: _____ Date: _____

Title: _____

What Is Expected	What Was Achieved
Student Success and Motivation Goals:	**Results:**
Career awareness video shown by all teachers	80% complete; remainder to be done in next month
Interest/skill assessment administered by teachers	Expectations met
Prioritization of interest videos, assessments by teachers	Expectations met; continued motivation required
Matching assessments to career awareness to show student relevance	Expectations met
Overall student motivation based on perceived relevance of education	Expectations met; ongoing progress needed
Individual student language assessments	75% accomplished; complete grades 2–4
Individual student math assessments	Expectations met for all grades
Measurement of incremental student progress by teacher	Needs improvement; as a whole, teachers are still teaching to a middle-range class level; lesson planning and methods need to be improved to prioritize more individualized learning
Results of individual student skill mastery—language	Expectations met
Results of individual student skill mastery—math	Expectations met
Academic Support Goals:	**Results:**
Volunteer tutor screening program	Exceeds expectations; very thorough
Number of volunteers recruited—3 per classroom	Average is 2 per classroom; making progress
Volunteer tutor effectiveness	Good; ongoing training required to improve effectiveness
After-school tutoring program effectiveness	Evaluation in process
Student skill mastery progression	Expectations met
Positive impact of tutoring on student skill mastery progression	Exceeds expectations. Individual student attention is helping tremendously

Learning Styles, Methods, State Standards Goals:	Results:
Administration of learning style tests	Expectations met
Results of learning style tests reported	Expectations met
Lesson plans to reflect 90% state standard content instruction	Expectations met
Classroom delivery to reflect 90% state standard content instruction	Expectations met
Lesson plans to reflect multimodal instruction	Needs improvement; most plans are auditory and visual only
Classroom delivery reflecting multimodal instruction	Needs improvement; most instruction is too auditory focused
Technology usage to reinforce content by individual student	Needs improvement; more time at computer lab needs to be integrated into lesson planning
Monthly test administration to determine student content mastery and progression to next concept	Exceeds expectations; great job managing all teachers to this goal

Community Connection Goals:	Results:
Overall community involvement by principal	Exceeds expectations; great job reaching out to all key organizations
Service organization involvement by principal	Expectations met
Local assisted-living site visits—3 per year	Expectations met
Local business visits to show educational relevance—3 per year	Below expectations; none so far this year
Museum visits for cultural experience—2 per year	Expectations met
Student application of community visits through writing assignments	Exceeds expectations; great student writing
Coordination of goal to involve community	Good progress being made
Coordination, recruitment of resources to assist paid staff	Expectations met; tutors are being added monthly

Administrative Goals:	Results:
Staff development weekly trainings	Expectations met
Overall communication	Exceeds expectations; great communication skills shown
Management of office staff resources	Expectations met
Adherence to budget objectives	Expectations met
Application of technology	Needs improvement; greater emphasis can be given to staff
4-hour response to voice mail	Expectations met
8-hour response to e-mail	Expectations met
Reaction to emergency situations	Exceeds expectations in coordinating 2 student injury situations

Manager's Comments

Employee's Comments

Signatures

Name	Title	Date
Employee: _____	_____	_____
Supervisor: _____	_____	_____

Next Meeting Date: _____

A performance discussion needs to have written closure. The sections for the manager's comments and employee's comments serve this purpose. Both the manager and subordinate put their thoughts in writing to confirm their communication. This also provides a documentation trail should there be a difference of opinion later on.

The signature box is a helpful final step in closing the meeting. It serves as a written confirmation that you have met, discussed the performance areas, and had the opportunity to provide written comments. The "Next Meeting Date" line enables you to schedule a date and time for your next performance discussion and put it on your calendar.

The monthly expectations document is an easy-to-use administrative tool to give objective feedback to those you manage. You can also use it as an agenda for performance reviews instead of creating another document for this purpose.

Job Description for LGLO Specialty Shoe Store

The following job description is for a store manager at LGLO. As with the Acme School District example, you can see that several key goals are highlighted as the essential duties and responsibilities.

Title: Store Manager
Location: Vista, CA
Type: Salaried Full Time

Company Description
LGLO Specialty Shoe Store is a unique retail store that specializes in helping people with foot, ankle, knee, and back pain. With an advanced technological approach, LGLO has assisted thousands of customers to feel better and improve their lives physically, emotionally, and mentally. LGLO is part of an internationally recognized franchise network with the highest ethical standards. Its owners, managers, and employees represent a highly trained staff with certified pedorthists who can effectively diagnose foot, ankle, knee, and back pain based on individual customer symptoms.

General Summary
The store manager is responsible for maintaining a positive relationship with new and repeat clients because customer satisfaction is the key to LGLO's success. The store manager role requires solid interpersonal communication skills, store management experience, financial acumen, and entrepreneurship.

Essential Duties and Responsibilities
- Develop and nurture the LGLO customer database.
- Develop programs to leverage referrals from the customer base.
- Gain repeat business from the customer base.
- Audit and manage overall customer satisfaction daily.
- Maintain an inviting store environment.
- Manage store inventory.
- Manage and motivate two to three store employees effectively.
- Promote teamwork among store employees to nurture the environment and maximize sales opportunities.
- Provide development paths and advancement opportunities for store employees.
- Oversee daily, weekly, monthly, and annual financial metrics and profitability.
- Show entrepreneurship and risk-reward behavior in the context of the LGLO mission and goals.
- Become a part of and represent LGLO in the local community.

Required Experience
- Advanced retail managerial skills with a demonstrated track record.

- Three to five years of experience managing in a retail store environment.
- Industry knowledge relative to the foot care and retail shoe business.
- Proven profit and loss balance sheet success in retail environment.

Required Education
- Bachelor's degree preferred

LGLO Store Manager Monthly Expectations

Based on the LGLO store manager job description, the following document lists monthly expectations and shows what a particular manager achieved. The document was created by the store manager's supervisor to provide feedback for a monthly performance review.

As in the Acme example, the first column lists specific key goals in five sections. Each of these sections has key tasks that comprise LGLO's plans to achieve the goals. By measuring the achievement of these tasks monthly, management is assured that the store manager's work aligns with the key plans to accomplish the LGLO mission.

Name: _____ Date: _____

Title: _____

What Is Expected	What Was Achieved
Customer Satisfaction Goals:	**Results:**
Verbal satisfaction questions for every customer by all store staff	Expectations met
Customer satisfaction survey mailed on the 1st of each month	Needs improvement; survey mailing is sporadic
Phone calls as follow-up to customer satisfaction survey within a week of mailer	Needs improvement; calls not being made on time
Cleanliness of store environment	Expectations met
Friendliness of store environment	Exceeds expectations; very friendly, family oriented
Overall positive store environment	Expectations met
Sales/Financial Goals:	**Results:**
Referral business for month: goal = $20,000	Slightly below expectations: $19,000
Repeat business for month: goal = $15,000	Expectations met: $16,000
New customer business for month: goal = $25,000	Below expectations: $ 12,500
Weekly profitability metric: goal = $1,923	Expectations met
Monthly profitability metric: goal = $8,333	Expectations met
Annual profitability metric: goal = $100,000	TBD

Management Goals:	Results:
Effective management of store employees	Expectations met
Motivation of store employees	Expectations met
Fostering of teamwork	Expectations met
Development of store employees	In process
Ability of each employee to handle multiple customers simultaneously	Needs improvement; 1 of 3 is able to accomplish; need to put specific improvement plan in place for each employee
Daily specials being offered and sold effectively	Expectations met
Self-direction of each employee	In process
Pedorthist certification	Certification accomplished this month
Local community organization meeting attendance	Expectations met

Entrepreneurship Goals:	Results:
Overall risk-reward effort	Expectations met; willing to take risks to achieve goals
Visitation of top 10 diabetic Medicare doctors	Expectations met; 4 referrals this month
Visitation of next 40 diabetic Medicare doctors	In process
Promotion of diabetic Medicare program to store customers	Expectations met
Diabetic Medicare mailer to 500-person list	Not achieved this month; goal for next month
Visitation of top 50 local doctors to introduce referral program	Exceeds expectations; 15 referrals this month
Mailer to 150 local doctors	In process

Administrative Goals:	Results:
Overall communication	Exceeds expectations
Utilization of technology	Could improve in this area
2-hour responsiveness to customer phone call	Expectations met
4-hour responsiveness to customer e-mails	Expectations met
Timely processing of employee timecards	Expectations met
Timely expense submittals	Expectations met

Manager's Comments

Employee's Comments

Signatures

Name	**Title**	**Date**
Employee: _____	_____	_____
Supervisor: _____	_____	_____

Next Meeting Date: _____

Recruiting

Good job descriptions and expectations are an essential part of recruiting new people for your team. The best recruiting tool you have is your personal and professional network. Recruiting and placement, whether for volunteers or employees, can involve a lot of risk. The optimal way to reduce risk is to recruit someone you know well or who is referred by someone you trust.

When recruiting, remember that you are trying to project a candidate's success in a particular role. Too often, managers get hung up on a person's resume and related experience. While asking specific questions about a person's background is important, seeing how the person's experiences and skills can be projected to the position you are recruiting for is even more critical. Remember that the interview process is a mutual activity. You are ultimately trying to determine a long-term fit for both your organization and the candidate.

Look for transferable skills that fit the profile of the job description. In most instances, candidates are required to have certain base-level credentials before they can be interviewed. However, once this base level is satisfied, you should look for skills that fit the prescribed role. Avoid the experience trap. One candidate may have experience in a particular field, but could another candidate who does not have the experience actually be better for the organization? Ultimately, you are looking for a candidate's long-term motivation, commitment, character, and skill set. Many candidates from outside a particular field can be great choices with the proper training and development.

As a result, it's better to recruit from a broad range of sources. Your goal is to put together a team with complementary members who can achieve organizational goals. Most times, a homogeneous group will not bring out the fresh ideas you need to be successful.

Once you have determined who is in the candidate pool and have received profile information, send the candidates your own resume and management philosophies before a first interview. This will help determine potential matches and gaps and enable you to gauge a candidate's preparation in advance of his or her initial conversation with you.

Interviewing

When the interview process begins, you should prepare before meeting the candidates. Make notes on the resumes or profiles about relevant experience, transferable skills, longevity, and so on. You can ask candidates a host of questions, but it is better to focus on questions related to how the candidates process information. Also ask questions about how they collaborate and work in group environments because this will give you an insight into their team orientation. Have they worked in collaborative environments before? How do they work in diverse group settings?

During the interviews tune into both the content of the answers and the candidates' poise in answering tough questions. Do they have the competitiveness and inner desire to achieve goals? Do they ask intelligent questions during the course of the conversation?

A minimum of three interviews with the manager is recommended for the candidates you're interested in, in addition to interviews with others in the organization. Use the first interview to determine a mutual long-term fit. Discuss the person's resume in detail, and focus on previous experience and transitions between jobs or volunteer positions. Questions and discussion about why a candidate left previous organizations or employers can give you valuable insight into that person's character.

Ask candidates if they received your profile information and if they have any questions about you or your organization. Ask if they have reviewed your management philosophies and what they think of them. This questioning will give you a worthwhile understanding of the candidate's level of preparation, ability to extrapolate information, and overall communication skills.

Use the second interview session to gauge candidates' motivation, enthusiasm, commitment, integrity, and work ethic. This discussion should center on the candidates' strengths and weaknesses, transferable skills, intellect, and ability to learn what is required. In this second interview, ask lots of open-ended questions to gauge the candidates' thought process and how they express themselves verbally. Frame the discussion around both professional and personal goals to get them to open up and to find out about their passions. Intelligent questions from candidates can help you predict their ability to absorb the intricacies of the job and help you gauge how they will assimilate into their prospective role.

In the third interview, focus on predicting the candidates' success in the specified role. Questions should center on job or role specifics. It is wise to have candidates submit a written plan and describe how they would approach the job or role if selected. This will give you insight into whether they have the applicable job, presentation, and thinking skills needed for success. Throughout the process, assess the candidates' proactive communication and enthusiasm because these usually are a good predictor of how the candidates will behave if selected.

To evaluate candidates' written communication skills, always require some type of written follow-up letter or e-mail. If the job or role entails a great deal of phone work, have at least one interview by phone to determine how a candidate projects over the telephone.

Additionally, candidates should meet as many managers and potential peers as possible so they understand your organization and the role they are pursuing. This also allows the organization to get many evaluations of the candidates. Ask people in your organization to be brutally honest with candidates about the team, position, and you as a manager. This will ensure full disclosure of the organization's culture and expectations should the candidate join the team. Candidates must know the good, bad, and ugly before walking in the door the first day. This will prevent any surprises and help to ensure a successful entry into your organization.

Ultimately, every manager is looking to recruit, interview, and bring on winners, not just survivors. A good vetting process will help both you and candidates evaluate long-term mutual fit and satisfaction.

The next sections will walk you through the three-step interview process, highlighting preparation, key questions to ask, and a suggested format for working through a resume. The resume examples are matched to the job descriptions and expectations for Acme and LGLO. They are provided to illustrate how to work through a candidate's resume and how to facilitate the interview process to best predict a candidate's success in the role.

Resume Example: Acme School District

This is the resume of Greg Klass, who is applying to be a principal in the Acme School District. After you have read the resume, turn to the next section to put yourself in the shoes of a manager interviewing him for this position.

GREG KLASS
330 Broadway Drive, Vista, CA 92051

Experience

1/1/2004–Present   Golden Elementary School, Vista, CA
                        Principal

Position entails oversight of 1,000-student elementary school in metropolitan school district. School staff includes 35 teachers and 3 administrative assistants. Implemented innovative test and assessment program to improve student test scores an average of 20% over a 5-year period. Focused on staff development in areas such as technology and methodology diversity.

1/1/2000–12/31/2003   Lincoln Elementary School, Lagress, TX
                       Assistant Principal

Responsible for administrative details of this 500-student school. Duties included attendance reporting, school district interface, student discipline, and budget oversight. Additional responsibilities in classroom observation and teacher development. School was recognized as one of nation's top 100 in 2002.

1/1/1996-12/31/1999   Beckwith Software, Dallas, TX
                       Regional Director

Position encompassed regional management of all facets of a $25 billion software company. Primary responsibilities included managing 25-person team relative to sales, engineering, administration, and resource allocation. Worked extensively with executives at Fortune 500 companies to implement software that improved workflow and productivity. Recognized as top region in 1998.

Education
MA, Educational Administration, University of Texas
BA, Business Administration, University of Texas

Volunteer Experience
Big Brothers of America, Mentor/Tutor
United Way, Development Committee

The Acme First Interview

Imagine now that you are considering Greg Klass for a principal position in the Acme School District. In preparation for the first interview, it is wise to do a quick review of the school site principal job description and expectations so they are fresh in your mind. When setting the appointment for the first interview, give the candidate your organization's website and pertinent information so he can prepare properly. Also, send your resume and personal management philosophies for the candidate to review.

The suggested length for the first interview is one hour. The suggested format is for you to ask questions for thirty to forty minutes and then allow the candidate to ask questions for the remainder of the allotted time. In this interview, you and the candidate are trying to gauge a potential long-term fit for both parties and whether or not it makes sense to have further conversations. You should also try to assess the candidate's intangible qualities. For example, is an honest dialogue occurring, or is the candidate just telling you what he thinks you want to hear?

In every first interview, you are really trying to understand the candidate's professional experience and personal story. When beginning the interview, ask questions about the candidate's background that may not be on the resume. The best way to understand the candidate's story is to work in chronological order. For example, ask candidates about where they grew up and what high school they attended. Then ask about their volunteer organizations and post-high-school education. This technique serves a twofold purpose. It brings out non-career-oriented information and also puts the candidate at ease because you don't dive right into job-related experience.

Another key focus area in a first interview is the candidate's transitions between jobs. Asking why a candidate left one job to take another can give you valuable insight into a candidate's commitment and thought process. Solid candidates usually have very good explanations for their movements.

When you review Greg Klass's resume for the first interview, you can see that he has several attributes that match the principal job description/expectations. In addition, some areas of concern need to be audited. Greg has the requisite master's and bachelor's degrees, and the fact that he has both public- and private-sector experience is a huge plus. Because Acme relies heavily on principals to do school site business management, Greg's experience in operations and financial management at Beckwith Software is great.

In his stint at Lincoln Elementary School, Greg was part of a team with extraordinary accomplishments as evidenced by the school being recognized as one of the nation's top 100. He appears to have been an integral part of this team as he had several key responsibilities. In his principal position at Golden Elementary School, Greg was able to implement innovative initiatives to advance student learning on an individual basis as evidenced by the increase in test scores. These accomplishments transfer nicely to Acme's emphasis on innovative ideas and a focus on individual student progress.

In the first interview, ask Greg open-ended questions and specific follow-up questions to elicit detailed answers as to how initiatives and plans were executed. Also, ask general questions as to how his experiences could translate to the Acme principal position.

In regard to potential areas of concern, the first to be audited is Greg's geographic movement. Although our societies are mobile, hiring a candidate who may not be committed to a particular geographic region can be risky. Remember that as a manager you are trying to predict a long-term fit. A host of risks and issues are associated with geographic movement, such as social foundation, cost of living, cultural adaptability, lifestyle pace, family ties, and so on. In addressing geographic concerns, be very straightforward with the candidate.

Another potential concern in Greg's resume is his long-term commitment to education. The fact that he has switched careers can be viewed as both good and bad. Questions about the career change and his commitment to the field of education should also be straightforward. Other than those two areas, this candidate has several skills and experiences that fit the Acme job description/expectation profiles.

Resume Example: LGLO Specialty Shoe Store

This resume is for a candidate who is applying for the position of store manager at LGLO Specialty Shoe Store.

KAREN WRANGLER
240 Marigold Lane, San Diego, CA 92121

Business Experience

1/1/2007–Present	Shoes for Less, San Diego, CA
	Store Manager

Position encompasses oversight of all store-related operations for this national franchise, including staff management, finances, inventory, and profit and loss. Duties also include forecasting and sales responsibilities for this $750,00-a-year store. Additional duties in marketing materials development and target market distribution. Achieved sales and profit and loss targets for last 5 years.

1/1/2001–12/31/2005   Boston Candy Store, San Diego, CA
                      Assistant Manager

Responsible for supporting the store manager with a variety of tasks, including store maintenance, sales, administration, inventory, and supply ordering. Experience working with candy manufacturers and distributors. Above average performance reviews each year.

1/1/1995–12/31/2000   Case Manager Social Worker, San Diego, CA
                      County of San Diego, Dept. of Social Services

Position entailed visitation and looking after the needs of 100 people as assigned by the County of San Diego Department of Social Services. Duties included visiting and determining services needed, such as food, clothing, housing, and transportation for clients. Received numerous honors and recognition, including Employee of the Year in 1998.

Education
AA, Social Services Work, Admont Community College
BA, Sociology (classes in progress), San Diego State University

Volunteer Experience
San Diego Boys and Girls Club, Mentor
St. John's Church, Third Grade Sunday School Teacher

The LGLO First Interview

In reviewing the resume for Karen Wrangle, you can see several skill sets and experiences that apply to the store manager position. She does not have the requisite educational background, but LGLO ownership has determined that she has enough qualifications to move forward with the interview process. As you move from bottom to top on the resume, you can see no geographical concerns because Karen has lived in the area her entire life. Her volunteer affiliations and recognition in the field of social work attest to her empathy for people, which is a strong intangible required by LGLO. Karen also has relevant experience in the other two positions she listed on her resume.

The concern areas are twofold. First, would she be committed to LGLO long term, or would she want to go back into government social work? This can be audited in the first interview. Second, the resume shows a one-year gap between the Boston Candy Store and Shoes for Less jobs. This is a somewhat common occurrence and can be attributed to a variety of issues such as store closings, bankruptcy, personnel changes, or family matters. When you see gaps on a resume, treat the discussion similarly to job transitions. A story is associated with each resume gap or change, and you need to question the candidate about it so you can gain a clear understanding of the circumstances. In this case, the manager has determined that the gap is not a big problem and that the candidate should proceed with the next steps.

Continuing the Interview Process

Before proceeding to the second part of the first interview, try to make sure you have asked all the detailed questions pertaining to the resume. However, if you don't feel like you have covered all the critical areas but you're running short on time, you can always address them in the second interview with the candidate.

In the second part of the first interview, you should allow the candidate to ask questions about your organization and the prospective position. A candidate's insightful questions will help you assess the person's intellect. You can also determine how much homework the candidate has done prior to the interview. This is also the time to see if the candidate has any questions about your background or management philosophies. Remember that when you discuss your management philosophies you are not looking for a candidate who agrees 100 percent but rather for the compatibility from which to develop a partnership.

If you decide you would like to bring the candidate back for a second interview, ask the candidate to send you a written summary of the first interview. The summary will help you assess the candidate's written communication skills and ensures a common understanding of what was discussed.

If you need time to think more about whether or not you will grant a second interview, tell the candidate you will get back to him or her within a week. If you know you do not want to proceed with a second interview, tell the candidate that you don't believe his or her experience or skill set is a fit for the position. All candidates should be told the truth at this point because they have invested time in the process and you don't want them to leave the interview with any misconceptions. Too many managers waste time by giving candidates false hope after the first interview. It is a sign of emotional strength to have the courage to tell people that you won't be hiring them and not hide behind others in the organization or use voice mail or e-mail to do it.

Prior to the second interview, you should send the candidate the job description and expectations documents. (The expectations document should have content in the first column only.) The second interview should be an hour and a half to two hours in length. Begin by discussing the candidate's summary of the first meeting. The job descriptions and expectations provide a good agenda for the rest of the second interview. Ask questions pertaining to the documents and work through them methodically to gauge a fit between the candidate and the role.

This part of the interview process is the most difficult because you are trying to discern the candidate's motivation, enthusiasm, commitment, integrity, and work ethic. Shifting between discussions of how the candidate's skill set matches the expectations and discernment of intangibles requires a great deal of finesse on your part. The expectations-matching discussion should be straightforward. You can go down the list of what is expected and ask the candidate to equate past experience and skills to the responsibilities.

However, the questions to gauge a candidate's intangibles are more difficult in that you are trying to discern the person's thought process as well as answers. Questioning techniques should be open ended and designed to evaluate the candidate's ability to think under pressure. Questions to discern motivation and enthusiasm include, "What makes you tick?" and, "What gets you up in the morning?"

Commitment is best audited by going back to the first interview questions about job transitions. Here you are looking to make sure the candidate's response as to why he or she made changes is consistent. Work ethic questions include, "What does your typical workday look like?" and, "How do you know when you're done for the day?" Integrity is best audited by asking a candidate to relate a couple of scenarios where he or she was put in a difficult ethical situation either person-ally or professionally and how the issue was solved. Be sure to ask these questions without giving the candidate a chance to prepare an answer because the spontaneous responses will typically give you good insight into the person's thought process and character.

Once the first two steps of the interview process are complete, you will have examined the candidate's skills, experience, and potential with the job description/expectations. Hopefully, you will have gleaned enough insight into the candidate's personality, character, and intan-gibles to assess if you want to continue the process. If you still have questions, address them before moving to the third interview.

The third interview is for predicting a candidate's success in the specified role. Prior to the meeting, ask the candidate to review all pub-lic information on your organization and the job description/expecta-tions and to present a written plan on how he or she would approach the role, if selected. This plan need only be a one-to-two-page bulleted synopsis to set the agenda for the third discussion. Begin the third interview by asking the candidate to present the plan to you. This gives you a thorough picture of the person's approach to the position. Any misconceptions about the job can be addressed during this time.

If the third interview goes well, it is a good time to discuss com-pensation in general terms. In addition, set up interviews with other managers and the candidate's potential peers so all the candidate's ques-tions can be answered and the expectations thoroughly understood. If input from the managers and peers is positive, you can move on to the candidate's references. A good practice is to call the references yourself and ask specific questions about how they think the candidate would do in the role. If you are satisfied with the reference checks and internal organizational feedback, you can feel confident you have done your due diligence to bring the candidate into your organization.

Hiring and Orientation

Just as you must take a calculated approach to interviewing and recruiting, you must also prepare thoroughly for the entrance of a new person into your organization. When bringing in a new person, fol-low the same principles described in the interviewing section. The key principle is that expectations need to be set properly and communicated regularly.

We have all been through the experience of entering a new organization or environment. We have felt both excitement and nervousness about the situation and what the future will bring. This energy is best channeled by showing the new person a road map of what the first few weeks will look like.

Begin by writing the successful candidate a letter right after the decision has been made that he or she will join your organization. This letter should welcome the individual to the organization and should clearly and specifically spell out the first two to three weeks of expectations and required activities. Highlighting expectations can greatly reduce any anxiousness and will help the new person feel comfortable joining your organization.

The letter should identify who will help smooth the person's transition into the organization. These people should be a combination of organizational resources and local mentors. Assign mentors who are presently performing the role satisfactorily, have done it in the past, or have detailed knowledge of the role.

The letter should also contain a day-by-day list of the tasks the new individual should accomplish in the first two or three weeks. These tasks should be as specific as possible and should relate to the mission and goals of the organization. In this way you will show a pattern of proper organizational priorities.

In addition to providing a task list, meet every other day with the new person and review the job description and expectations document for the role in detail. This will set the new hire on the correct path. Good performers will start to own the role within the first two weeks and should begin to achieve tasks that exceed the expectations outlined in the welcome letter. Your number one responsibility in the first couple of weeks is to get new people settled into their roles, help them gain confidence, and set them up for success. We have all experienced the opposite, which is being thrown to the wolves. Bringing in new people and letting them fend for themselves is not productive. It is, however, beneficial to allow them two-day increments to achieve their tasks without micromanagement. This approach can give you good insight into how they will attack the expectations of their job description, as well as their work ethic, personal organization skills, and thought processes.

As part of the welcome letter, you should also introduce a ninety-day plan with a checklist that specifies expectations for that period. This plan ought to encompass training, organizational knowledge, specific role development plans, and so on. The ninety-day plan needs to expand on the welcome letter and integrate the heart of the job description and expectations into an easy-to-follow checklist format.

After ninety days you should have a pretty good idea of how new people fit their roles, what their areas of strength and weakness are, and how they should be managed day to day, week to week, and month to month. Now it is time to take the training wheels off the bike and see how they perform. Take into account that we all make mistakes, especially during the ramp-up period. Look at these mistakes as part of the learning process. As mentioned previously, you are responsible for setting new hires up for success. If you lay the proper foundation and expectations, you can accomplish this within the first ninety days.

Following are examples of welcome letters and ninety-day checklists that illustrate the above concepts. You can create more detailed letters and plans by simply adding more tasks to the format.

Welcome Letter, Acme School District

The candidate we met in the interview process was chosen for the principal job. Here is the welcome letter he received.

Date: September 4, 2016
To: Greg Klass
From: Superintendent, Acme School District
cc: Acme School Board, Acme District Personnel
Subject: Welcome Aboard

Dear Greg,

We are excited about your joining the Acme School District on Monday, September 12. I have copied the school board and district personnel on this letter. This is intended as a road map for the first two weeks so you know what to expect. Principal Jay North of Avid Elementary School will be your mentor. He will be working with you on a daily basis to help smooth your entry into the Acme School District.

General

Our ongoing district schedule includes a meeting at the district headquarters for all principals at 3:30 p.m. on Mondays. Principals are also required to attend school board meetings, which are held the third Tuesday of each month at 7:00 p.m. in the district office.

September 12

- 8:00 a.m.: Be introduced to teaching staff at school preparation day.
- 10:00 a.m.: Attend new hire orientation at the district office.
- Noon: Have lunch with your principal mentor, Jay North.
- Get settled into your office.
- Call other district principals to introduce yourself.

September 13

- Review *District Policy and Procedure Handbook*.
- Familiarize yourself with the district website.
- Set up your technical tools: e-mail, office phone, cell phone, and so on.
- Set up your home office technical tools.
- Continue introductory calls to district principals.

September 14

- Shadow mentor Jay North for the day.

September 15

- Continue to settle into your office and school site.
- Schedule district office appointments for September 16 with Helen Baker, Human Resources; George Michaels, Payroll; Beth Nordstrom, Curriculum; Joe Fish, Business Operations; and Karen Smiley, School Board President.

September 16

- Attend above appointments at district office.

September 19

- Preside over first day of school.
- Greet students and parents as they arrive.
- Work through any logistical issues that arise.
- Continue tasks from previous week.

September 20

- Prepare for faculty meeting on September 21 to reinforce the Acme School District mission, goals, and plans.
- Preview career awareness video for presentation at the faculty meeting.
- Preview the interest/skills assessment for presentation at the faculty meeting.
- Prepare presentation for the faculty meeting showing how to match the career awareness video and interest/skills assessment.
- Attend school board meeting.
- Normal school routine.

September 21

- 3:00 p.m.: Attend faculty meeting; present September 20 content you have developed.
- Prepare student language and math assessment program for distribution to faculty.
- Meet with staff office personnel to discuss logistics, improvements, and adjustments for the second week of school.
- Begin formulating tutoring programs.
- Normal school routine.

September 22

- Distribute student language and math assessment programs to the teachers.
- Check teacher lesson plans for the week.
- Do half-hour classroom observations for the three new teachers.
- Ensure all technology is functional throughout the school.
- Conduct normal school routine.

September 23

- Make initial contact with service organizations and businesses to set appointments for the following week.
- Meet with Parent-Teacher Association president.
- Ensure all tasks in this letter have been accomplished.
- Conduct normal school routine.

Acme School District Principal Ninety-Day Checklist

This checklist takes the new principal through his first ninety days on the job.

30-DAY CHECKLIST

____*Attend principal meetings.*

____*Attend board meetings.*

____*Attend ongoing meetings with mentor—four per month.*

____*Meet with all district principals.*

____*Gain a thorough understanding of Acme policy and procedures.*

____*Gain a thorough understanding of Acme website and technology tools.*

____*Meet with district personnel from Human Resources, Payroll, Curriculum, and Business Operations.*

____*Meet with school board president.*

____*Manage all aspects of school site operations successfully.*

____*Attend weekly faculty meetings.*

____*Reinforce Acme School District mission, goals, and plans with faculty.*

____*Conduct weekly office staff meetings.*

____*Conduct weekly checks of teacher lesson plans to ensure adherence to state standards content and methodology variety.*

____*Ensure technology is functional and being utilized throughout the school.*

____*Meet with service organizations and businesses.*

____*Set student field trip schedule for year.*

____*Set student volunteer schedule for year to include assisted living, senior center, hospitals, and so on.*

____*Attend monthly meeting with Parent-Teacher Association president.*

____*Oversee administration of learning style test to each student.*

____*Ensure career awareness video is shown to each student.*

60-DAY CHECKLIST

____*Ensure all students finish their interest/skill assessment.*

____*Ensure the monthly language and math assessments are being accomplished.*

____*Ensure after-school tutoring programs are operational.*

___*Ensure matching of the skill assessment results and career awareness choices is done to illustrate relevance to schoolwork.*

___*Oversee monthly measurement of incremental student progress by teachers.*

___*Ensure volunteer tutoring program is operational.*

___*Ensure results of learning style tests are incorporated into individual student oriented instruction.*

___*Ensure lesson plans reflect 90 percent state standard content.*

___*Ensure instruction to reflect 90 percent state standard content.*

___*Inspect teacher utilization of technology to reinforce content for students.*

___*Attend service organization events weekly to foster community connection.*

___*Conduct weekly staff development trainings.*

90-DAY CHECKLIST

___*Conduct three-month measurement of incremental student progress by teachers.*

___*Conduct three-month measurement of individual student skill mastery in language and math.*

___*Monitor and adjust volunteer tutoring program.*

___*Ensure teacher adherence to learning style and methodology variety in lesson plans and classroom instruction.*

___*Conduct three-month measurement of state standard content being taught by teachers.*

___*Conduct three-month assessment of effectiveness of multimodal lesson planning and instruction.*

___*Conduct monthly one-on-one meetings with all staff members to go over their individual expectations.*

___*Facilitate the involvement of the community in school instruction, events, and activities.*

___*Oversee coordination and recruitment of volunteer resources to assist in achieving the Acme School District mission, goals, and plans.*

___*Ensure monthly adherence to budget objectives.*

___*Be responsive to students, teachers, and parents.*

Welcome Letter, LGLO Specialty Shoe Store

Karen Wrangler, whose resume we saw in the previous section, was hired as a manager at LGLO. Here is the welcome letter she received. It describes her first two weeks in her new job.

Date: January 2, 2008
To: Karen Wrangler
From: LGLO Specialty Shoe Store Ownership
Subject: Welcome Aboard

Dear Karen,

We are excited about your joining LGLO on Monday, January 15. This letter is intended as a road map for your first two weeks so you know what to expect. As owner and interim manager of LGLO, I will serve as your mentor. I will work with you on a daily basis to help smooth your entry into the LGLO Specialty Shoe Store manager role.

General

LGLO weekly staff meetings are held Tuesday and Friday at 9:00 a.m. prior to the store opening at 10:00 a.m. These are mandatory for all personnel. As manager, you will be leading these sessions after your first two weeks.

January 15

- 9:00 a.m.: Attend orientation with store ownership.
- 9:30 a.m.: Meet with store staff.
- Receive in-depth overview from store ownership of public-facing store duties and back-office duties.
- Get settled into the manager's office.
- Observe staff-customer interactions.
- Meet with ownership to discuss benefits, payroll, and so on.

January 16

- Review the *LGLO Specialty Shoe Store Handbook and Operations Guide.*
- Familiarize yourself with the LGLO website.
- Review the customer base.
- Review profit and loss statements from the previous two years.
- Learn the daily store opening and closing procedures.

January 17
- 10:00 a.m.: Open store to the public.
- Learn the technology tools, including computer software and point-of-sale system.
- Learn how to operate the store's foot diagnostic machine.
- Review and study the 10-step selling methodology.
- Observe staff during store hours.
- Learn all store product lines.

January 18
- 10:00 a.m.: Open store.
- Schedule January 19 visit to San Diego LGLO franchise.
- Review the repeat business data for the previous two years.
- Review the referral business data for the previous two years.
- 6:00 p.m.: Close store.

January 19
- Visit San Diego LGLO Specialty Shoe Store for the day.
- Spend the day observing and asking questions about store policies and procedures.
- Review job descriptions and expectations for each store employee.

January 22
- 10:00 a.m.: Open store.
- Meet with ownership to discuss and ask questions regarding the past week's activities.
- Continue to review profit and loss, repeat, and referral data.
- Engage customers on store floor, applying the 10-step selling methodology.
- 6:00 p.m.: Close store.

January 23
- Open and close store every day from this point forward.
- Begin directing store staff based on individual job descriptions and expectations.
- Begin customer satisfaction survey mailer program.
- Assess and adjust store environment when appropriate.

January 24
- Hold one-on-one meetings with all employees to reinforce their job descriptions and expectations.
- Continue customer satisfaction survey mailer program.
- Assess and adjust store environment.

January 25
- Schedule service organization attendance for January 26.
- Assess store employee teamwork and skill sets.
- Plan and schedule top 10 diabetic Medicare doctor visits to introduce the Medicare program.
- Plan and schedule top 50 local doctor visits to introduce the referral program.

January 26
- Begin leading staff meetings.
- Attend service organization meeting.
- Develop diabetic Medicare mailer.
- Continue to accomplish above activities.

LGLO Specialty Shoe Store Manager Ninety-Day Checklist

This checklist walks the new manager through her first ninety days.

30-DAY CHECKLIST

____*Preside over twice-weekly staff meetings.*
____*Attend weekly meeting with ownership.*
____*Gain thorough knowledge of store handbook.*
____*Gain thorough knowledge of operations guide.*
____*Open and close store daily.*
____*Gain thorough knowledge of foot diagnostic machine.*
____*Manage and apply the 10-step selling methodology.*
____*Gain working knowledge of all store product lines.*
____*Call/visit three other LGLO franchises to observe and learn best practices.*
____*Conduct weekly one-on-one meetings with staff to reinforce expectations.*
____*Become involved in the community.*

____*Promote the diabetic Medicare program to store customers.*
____*Accomplish all administrative goals.*

60-DAY CHECKLIST

____*Gain thorough knowledge of customer base.*
____*Ensure customer satisfaction verbal assessment, mailer, and phone calls become consistent.*
____*Upgrade and adjust store environment.*
____*Increase referral business month over month.*
____*Increase repeat business month over month.*
____*Apply weekly profitability metrics to increase overall profitability by 20 percent.*
____*Conduct employee teamwork and motivation assessment.*
____*Increase daily special sales conversion.*
____*Visit top 10 diabetic Medicare doctors.*

90-DAY CHECKLIST

____*Gain thorough knowledge of previous two years' profit and loss.*
____*Increase new customer business 10 percent month over month.*
____*Manage profit and loss.*
____*Increase profitability additional 15 percent annual rate.*
____*Conduct overall development of store employees.*
____*Ensure pedorthist certification completion by each employee.*
____*Visit top 50 diabetic Medicare doctors.*
____*Send diabetic Medicare mailer to 500-person list.*
____*Visit top 50 local doctors to introduce referral program.*
____*Send mailer to 150 local doctors.*

Your Organization's Information Base

The previous sections in this chapter focused on people within your organization. This section looks at people outside the organization. How do they find out about the organization? Is what they are reading or hearing what you want them to know?

Laying a common information base to the constituency you serve is vital to achieving your organization's mission. This means that every individual in the organization has to present the same basic message.

Unless you insist that organization members lay a common information base, individuals will communicate their own message as they understand it. This can lead to communication of a fragmented message to the market that can differ drastically from the organization's mission and goals.

The best way to achieve a common information base is to allot time to train all members inside the organization. Three informational pieces should be developed. The first is a company nugget, a maximum of two lines distilling the organization's mission, value, and differentiators. The nugget should clearly state what differentiates you from others relative to your mission.

The second piece is a more detailed synopsis, one to two paragraphs expanding on the organization's mission, goals, value, and differentiators. The third piece should be a more detailed and specific message with supporting content, statements, references, testimonials, and so on. It should be a detailed summary of the who, what, why, where, and how of accomplishing your mission and goals. This piece can be easily formulated by expanding ideas from the goals and plans.

Once developed, these pieces need to be adjusted and refined based on their effectiveness. All members of the organization must learn the pieces in detail, own their content, and be able to articulate them at a moment's notice. This may be somewhat difficult with the third piece, but the company nugget and synopsis have to be learned and ably communicated by *everyone* in the organization. Otherwise, the proper information base cannot be laid.

Once the appropriate training has been conducted internally, encourage all organization members to communicate the company nugget and synopsis to everyone they meet. This will accomplish the twofold purpose of getting the message out in the target community as advertising and also enabling organizational members to have a lot of practice telling the story.

Following are examples of the company nugget, synopsis, and detailed message for Acme and LGLO.

Acme School District Information Base

The nugget is typically the organization's mission statement or a combination of the mission statement and key goals. The Acme synopsis and detailed messages are presented in a bulleted format to illustrate how to build the three pieces in sequence and for application to a presentation medium.

NUGGET

As you may recall, the mission of the Acme School District is "Develop lifelong learners who can pursue academic achievement in their individual learning styles and are connected to the community." Here is how the mission statement has been rephrased to become the organization's nugget:

> The Acme School District's mission is to help students develop into lifelong learners. We provide an environment for students to pursue academic achievement in their individual learning styles and connect them to their community.

SYNOPSIS

The synopsis is developed from the organization's goals, which you can read on page 64. Unlike the nugget, Acme's synopsis barely changes the original wording of the goals.

- The Acme School District seeks to create an environment where students are motivated, achieve success, and enjoy learning.
- Acme provides an extensive academic support system that enables students to succeed to the best of their abilities.
- Acme utilizes a variety of methodologies and teaches subject matter in innovative ways to maximize student learning.
- Acme views the school district as a significant part of the community and strives to provide students opportunities to become part of it through a variety of experiences.

DETAILED MESSAGE

The detailed message should be developed from key internal resources, including organizational plans, rolling agendas, best practices, and so on. The best way to develop the detailed message is to provide information regarding the who, what, why, where, and how of achieving the mission. The detailed message expands and builds on the nugget and synopsis. It should contain references and testimonials to further enhance your organization's credibility.

Who

- Acme is a public elementary school district with 5,000 students.
- It is a forward-thinking organization that employs unique philosophies and methods.
- Acme believes that a shared responsibility for the over- all education of children belongs to parents, teachers, administrators, and the community at large.
- Acme intentionally promotes educational relevance in a variety of ways.
- Acme believes in having community volunteers assist in the academic and social development of its students.

What

- Acme develops students to become lifelong learners.
- Acme creates an environment in which students are moti- vated, achieve success, and enjoy learning.
- The district provides opportunities for students to explore areas of interest and pursue them.
- By finding interest areas and experiencing the success of advancement, students enjoy learning and are motivated to continue their education.
- State-standard-based content is presented in a variety of ways with heavy technology emphasis for reinforcement.
- All students are given an interest/skill assessment to iden- tify their strengths and areas of expertise.
- All students are shown career/job videos to broaden their awareness and promote educational relevance.
- Acme thoroughly screens and trains all classroom and field trip volunteers.
- State standards are the baseline for instruction and com- prise 90 percent of classroom time.

- Students apply what they have learned on field trips and community visits by completing writing assignments about them.

Why

- Acme believes each student has unique skills and learning styles and that student instruction should be as individualized as possible.
- Acme believes that the school district must provide the curriculum and framework necessary for individualized student education.
- Acme believes that students will enjoy learning and continue to be motivated if they experience academic progress and skill mastery.
- Students will benefit from a feeling of personal fulfillment when they serve in local community organizations.
- Acme seeks to broaden student awareness by providing a range of experiences outside the school setting.
- Acme provides students the opportunity to view career awareness videos and do an interest/skill assessment to show how they can apply their educational experiences in the future.

Where

- Acme has five schools in the San Diego, California, city limits.
- Acme intentionally connects its students' education to the community in which they live.
- Acme gives students the opportunity to become part of their community by serving in local organizations.
- Students visit local assisted-living facilities, businesses, and museums to gain an appreciation and awareness of their community.

How

- Acme emphasizes individual learning style development.
- Acme provides an academic support system that enables students to succeed to the best of their abilities.
- Acme provides a variety of methodologies to teach content in innovative ways to maximize student learning.
- The district assesses all students at their current language and math levels and develops programs for individual advancement.
- Additional academic support comes by utilizing community volunteers to help tutor students.
- Learning style tests are administered to determine how each student best learns.
- Instruction is given in audio, visual, and kinesthetic modes to make sure all students are taught in their best learning style.
- Assessments take place after each unit to make sure students have mastered state-standard-based content.
- Field trip and visits to a range of community venues take place both during and after school hours.
- Parents and community volunteers help supervise student field trips and visits.
- Teachers, aides, and volunteers match interest/skill assessments with career awareness choices to promote educational relevance to the students.
- Community volunteers are utilized for student tutoring programs.
- Individual assessments are given to gauge each student's math and language skill mastery level.
- Acme utilizes computer lab programs to reinforce content to students.
- Acme administers monthly tests to determine individual student progress and advance students to the next level when ready.

- Parent-Teacher Association members and community volunteers assist with community visits and tutoring.

Acme References and Testimonials

"Having observed hundreds of school districts in my 30 years of education, I was blown away by what the Acme School District is doing. Everyone is truly tending to each student's individual needs, and the kids are really motivated to learn."

Dottie Collision

NEA Today

"I have had the wonderful experience of tutoring these young children for over 5 years in the Acme School District. The teachers make me feel like a part of their staff. It is so fulfilling to see these kids progress in their grasp of their academics and life in general."

Cassandra Smith

Acme School District Volunteer Tutor

"As a new teacher in the Acme School District, I am very appreciative of this wonderful district and community support system. We really have the opportunity to see the kids master a concept before moving to another one. The career awareness and interest/skill program helps the students see what they can do with their education in the future."

Jim Craig

Acme School District Fifth-Grade Teacher

"I really like my teacher. She makes school fun. She teaches our subjects in a lot of different ways so I can understand them. I saw a video on being a doctor and that is what I want to be. I am going to do my homework."

Shalveen Selma

Acme School District Third-Grade Student

LGLO Specialty Shoe Store Information Base

The LGLO shoe store created the following information base.

NUGGET

The company's mission statement is this: "The mission of LGLO is to help people physically, educationally, and socially as a profitable company." Here is the company's nugget based on its mission:

LGLO's mission is to help people physically, educationally, and socially from a retail specialty shoe store location.

Synopsis

LGLO's synopsis is based directly on its goals. (See pages 56–57 for a complete list of the organization's goals.)

- LGLO's number one priority is customer satisfaction.

- LGLO's goal is to provide a positive and friendly store environment to which customers enjoy coming.

- LGLO seeks to educate its customers in good health practices through store interactions and by phone, e-mail, and mail.

- LGLO strives to create partnerships with its customers.

- LGLO values teamwork and ethics among its employees.

- LGLO is a highly involved part of its local community.

Detailed Message

The detailed message can be used for presentations, printed materials, the organization's website, media packets, and many other purposes.

Who

- LGLO's number one priority is customer satisfaction.

- LGLO seeks to provide a positive and friendly store environment to which customers enjoy coming.

- LGLO strives to create partnerships with its customers.

- LGLO values employee teamwork and motivation.

- LGLO is a highly ethical organization that believes in focusing on customer needs.

- LGLO is an involved part of its local community.

- LGLO employs a staff of well-trained and certified pedorthists.

What

- LGLO is a specialty shoe store that helps people physically, educationally, and socially.

- LGLO is a destination retail specialty shoe store.

- LGLO educates its customers and potential customers in good health practices.

- Store management evaluates employees by observing their self-motivation and whether they meet the store standard of going above and beyond expectations.
- LGLO provides daily low-priced specials to customers.
- LGLO specializes in diabetic patient foot care.
- LGLO partners with diabetic Medicare doctors to provide great service to customers.
- LGLO is a certified diabetic Medicare footwear provider.
- LGLO partners with local doctors to provide comprehensive foot care for patients.

Why

- Customer satisfaction is the number one priority, and it fulfills the mission.
- Satisfied customers refer others, which sustains the business.
- LGLO thrives when customers are satisfied and return for repeat purchases.

Where

- The store location is in Vista, California.
- It serves the communities of Vista, Oceanside, Carlsbad, San Marcos, and Escondido.

How

- LGLO educates its customers and potential customers in good health practices through in-store conversations.
- LGLO educates our customers and potential customers in good health practices through its website, phone conversations, e-mail, mail, and newsletters.
- LGLO motivates its employees by having compensation plans based on customer satisfaction.
- LGLO employees can build a stake in the organization by achieving customer satisfaction goals.

- LGLO measures customer satisfaction by verbally asking in-store customers and mailing a five-question survey to them after a store visit.
- Customer satisfaction is enhanced by providing a socially friendly store environment.
- The store staff calls each customer the day following a purchase to ensure satisfaction.
- The LGLO store staff uses a 10-step customer evaluation process to ensure the right product is recommended.
- The store staff typically spends thirty to forty-five minutes with each customer.

LGLO References and Testimonials

"I was able to be fitted with new shoes and support at very little cost through LGLO's diabetic foot care program. The staff really went the extra mile for me."

Lola Pierce
Oceanside, CA

"My experience with LGLO was phenomenal. They spent an hour with me to explain where my foot and knee problems come from and how they could help me. I am a satisfied customer and would recommend LGLO to others."

Vern Werner
San Marcos, CA

"When I got to the LGLO store I was walking with a limp and was stooped over. After working with the staff I was fitted with custom orthotics and a pair of unbelievably supportive shoes. I walked out of the store more upright then I've been in 10 years. It was a miracle."

Joe Blythe
Vista, CA

Quick Reference

This chapter focused on people within and outside the organization. It began with job descriptions because an organization can get off track easily if individuals do not follow their job descriptions. It introduced a calculated approach to interviewing and recruiting winners. Then, because bringing in new people and letting them figure out the job for themselves is not productive, we looked at the important task of orienting new hires to the team. Finally, this chapter explained how to lay an information base so that all members of the organization, regardless of role, give the same message about the organization and spread the word about it to everyone they meet.

Job Descriptions and Expectations

- You must make sure individual team members know their roles and tasks specifically and in detail.
- You need to develop expectations documents to measure performance against job descriptions and refer to them frequently.
- Expectation reviews are the only way to link back to the job description and give people truly objective insight into their performance.
- Clearly stated expectations minimize subjectivity in the feedback process and enable you to give direction to subordinates.

Recruiting

- The best recruiting tool you have is your personal and professional network because you reduce risk by recruiting people you know well or who are referred by someone you trust.
- When recruiting and interviewing, you are trying to determine a long-term fit for both your organization and the candidate.
- Ultimately, you are looking at a candidate's long-term motivation, commitment, character, and skill set.
- Once you have determined your candidate pool, you should send the candidates your own resume and management philosophies.

Interviewing

- During the interview, you need to tune into both the content of the answers and the candidate's poise in responding to questions.
- The first interview should be used to determine a mutual long-term fit and focus on the person's resume. The second interview should be used to gauge a candidate's motivation, enthusiasm, commitment, integrity, and work ethic.

- The third interview should focus on predicting the candidate's success in the specified role. Candidates should meet as many managers and potential peers as possible so they understand your organization and the role they are pursuing.

- You should always require some type of written follow-up letter or e-mail from the candidate to evaluate the candidate's written communication skills.

Hiring and Orientation

- Before a new hire starts, you should send him or her a letter that clearly spells out expectations and required activities for the first two to three weeks.

- You should assign a mentor who is performing or has performed the same role satisfactorily to meet every other day with the new person.

- As part of the welcome letter, you can introduce a ninety-day plan that specifies expectations for that period.

- After ninety days, you should have a good idea of how the new person fits the role and how he or she should be managed on a daily, weekly, and monthly basis.

Your Organization's Information Base

- The first piece of the information base is a company nugget, no more than two lines long, that distills the organization's mission, value, and differentiators.

- The second piece is a more detailed synopsis of one to two paragraphs that expands on the organization's mission, goals, value, and differentiators.

- The third piece, the detailed message, should contain supporting content, statements, references, testimonials, a value proposition, and so on.

- All members of the organization should learn the pieces in detail, own the content, and be able to articulate them at a moment's notice to everyone they meet.

CHAPTER 9

Learning Key
Administrative Skills

B EING A MANAGER means paying attention to detail. This chapter features some important administrative techniques you can use to manage in a productive manner. These administrative competencies focus on time and presentations by you or others. Using these powerful techniques every day will enable you to focus your attention on achieving your organization's mission.

Time Management

You need to plan your time strategically to maximize your focus on accomplishing your organization's mission, goals, and plans. Your activities should always be tied to your key initiatives. The following ideas may help you with overall time management and handling the multitude of tasks you face in your role.

Priorities

Set priorities based on your most important goals. Sort and prioritize your meetings, lessons, phone calls, voice-mails, e-mails, and so on, by importance. Give priority to the requests of your manager and executives. Initially, give lower priority to peer and subordinate requests unless you deem them to be strategic or critical. Remember that people always think their own issue is the most important and urgent.

Deal with nonpriority items superficially. If they become a priority, they will surface again.

Once you've prioritized your tasks, move them to your calendar as soon as possible.

Daily Routine

Do the tasks you don't like to do first and get them out of the way. Plan time gaps in each day for potential problems and short-notice activities. Try to work on your important long-term initiatives and plans each day so you aren't overwhelmed as deadlines approach. Spend 80 percent of your time on the most important 20 percent of tasks and plans.

Handle tasks quickly, but don't hurry the management of the key ones. Remember that busyness and high activity levels don't necessarily translate into execution and results. Busyness can bring a false sense of security—it doesn't mean priorities or objectives are being met. Make informed judgments and move forward without hesitation or overanalysis. You can adjust plans and tasks as you go.

Sharing the Load

Strive to develop partnerships and relationships as you accomplish routine tasks. Delegate and monitor whenever possible. Try to delegate the trivial administrative details to free up your time.

Messages

Remember that you don't always have to answer the phone. Letting people leave messages or voice mail is acceptable. This allows you to manage your activity and not have it manage you.

Filing

Make sure to have easily remembered electronic and paper filing systems so you can access information quickly and not waste time. Handle each piece of paper, message, e-mail, and voice mail once and file it appropriately. Be constantly ready to take in information and then file it to make sure you aren't missing anything.

Scheduling

Plan and adhere to weekly, monthly, and quarterly schedules. Always map out your plan for the next day before you leave work so you can begin executing it when you start the next day. If you try to organize your day first thing in the morning, you are already behind.

Schedule a weekly meeting time to discuss all important initiatives and plans with your team. Never conclude an important meeting or task without scheduling a date and time for follow-up.

Calendar Setting

A crucial part of time management is your calendar. Your calendar should directly reflect your priorities. Oftentimes your calendar and daily schedule can become overpopulated with nonpriority items. Be sure your calendar reflects all the tasks you need to accomplish to execute plans, achieve goals, and fulfill the organization's mission. You'll need to exhibit good discipline and good time management habits to make sure your calendar ties directly to accomplishing short- and long-term initiatives. In effect, your calendar is a puzzle and you have to schedule the key pieces first. Below are some administrative suggestions for effectively organizing your calendar.

Annual Calendar

Look at your calendar at the beginning of the year and enter key personal and professional dates first. Roll key dates on your calendar from year to year and build your schedule around them, if appropriate.

Quarterly Calendar

View your calendar at the beginning of each month and schedule critical dates for the next ninety days. Adjust the schedule on a monthly basis to accommodate changes. In your ninety-day outlook, make sure you have time designated to regularly evaluate progress on your mission, goals, and plans. Use the designated dates to reinforce the vital organizational and departmental initiatives with your team.

Monthly Calendar

Your monthly calendar is extremely important, so allot ample time to strategically plan each month. Put all standing meetings and personal appointments on the monthly calendar first. Make sure that all standing meetings directly relate to the accomplishment of plans.

At the beginning of each month, determine which objectives you must execute and make sure your calendar reflects this. Your priority tasks and actions have to make it onto your calendar or they will never be completed.

Weekly Calendar

Don't wait until Monday to confirm your weekly calendar; set it by Friday of the previous week. Always go into the week with a full calendar. Otherwise, too many nonpriorities will work their way onto your schedule.

Schedule some gaps in each day for unexpected items, and be sure to schedule time on your calendar after a key meeting or event so you can follow up while ideas and discussions are still fresh in your mind.

Note Taking

How well you follow up after a meeting or event can depend on your skill at taking notes. Fast-paced classes, meetings, and other events require you to develop a personalized system to capture information, process it, and act on it. In the information age, so much data is coming at you that you need to strategically figure out how to process it and extract what is important. You also need to have a note-taking system to recall and retrieve information because typically you will remember only a small percentage of what you see or hear.

In addition, whether you're attending a classroom lecture, business meeting, or event, taking notes shows speakers that you value what they are saying. Here are a few suggestions for taking notes effectively.

- Try to preview or anticipate the content that will be presented. This will get you mentally attuned to the discussion prior to the beginning of the session.
- Prior to taking notes, plan what you will need to do with the information and act accordingly. Taking notes for a final exam three months away is quite different from taking notes for a follow-up correspondence that is required the same day.

- When taking notes, focus on capturing only words or concepts that will help you reconstruct the content later. You can put together your full thoughts after the session.

- Always try to synthesize the information in your notes as it is being presented. This will help you recall and remember the information later.

- For easier organization later, divide your notes into sections, leaving plenty of empty space between different thoughts or subjects.

- Do a mental or written synopsis or recap immediately following the session so you can better retrieve the information from your notes.

Presentations

Sometimes other people will be taking notes while you do the talking. Here are some tips for being successful in presentations of all types.

The number one priority of presenters should be to convey their content in such a way that the audience can learn it, retain it, and apply it. All too often, presentations appear to be focused on the presenter merely getting through an abundance of information rather than communicating effectively to the audience.

Keep in mind that the audience will retain only a small portion of what is offered. Therefore, focus the presentation on three to five key points you would like the audience to learn, remember, and apply. State these key points in the introduction, reinforce them in the body of the presentation, and summarize them at the conclusion. In your introduction, communicate to the audience what you would like them to learn and why, and then follow up the presentation with a synopsis in electronic or paper format.

If you present too much information too quickly, the audience is likely to shut down and you will have wasted both their time and yours. Keep the presentation concise and move through it at a steady pace. Ask, "Are there any questions?" as you go. This will keep the audience engaged. Questions such as "Does that make sense?" or "Is that applicable?" will also help hold their attention.

Always be conscious of the engagement level of the audience. Monitor body language, facial expressions, note taking, and so on, to make sure two-way communication is occurring. Feel free to direct questions to the group as a whole and to individuals. Participants pay better attention when they know that the presenter may be calling on them. Research your audience and know their profile information so you can ask targeted questions that apply to their roles and responsibilities. Never present for more than thirty minutes without a break or scheduled time for interaction.

Presentation Tools

To create an effective presentation, you'll need to become comfortable using the most common presentation methods: computer or overhead projector; paper presentation; and whiteboard, chalkboard, or flip chart. This section offers some tips for handling these tools effectively.

COMPUTER OR OVERHEAD PROJECTION

Computer projection is the most popular method of presentation in most fields. It is combined with overhead projection in this section because both methods have the same characteristics. In both delivery methods, you face the audience with the device in front of you, so you can make eye contact with the audience while delivering the information. Besides being the most popular, the computer-based presentation method is the best for remote and remote/in-person hybrid environments. Below are a few suggestions for utilizing computer or overhead projection.

- *Room environment.* With projection, the room is typically darkened and the audience is focused on the projection screen. Use some type of lighting to keep people attentive. (This is particularly necessary after a meal.) Prior to presenting, ask the audience if everyone can see the screen. Make sure you do not stand in front of it or obstruct anyone's view.
- *Content format.* Focus your content on the three to five key points you want the audience to take away. Never place more than five to six sentences on each slide. Slides with too many points are difficult for the audience to see and difficult for the

presenter to present. Moving at a steady pace will help the presentation flow properly.

Realize that everyone in your audience is wondering how many slides will be presented. Most of us have had the experience of sitting through "death by PowerPoint" with endless numbers of slides that have too many sentences on each one. Remember that conciseness and brevity are signs of intelligence. Your slides should have ideas and concepts, not lengthy sentences. Eliminate any words that are not vital.

If the desired presentation is forty-five minutes to an hour, allow for audience participation to keep everyone engaged. Know your material thoroughly so it is familiar and you don't have to read it during the presentation. Make sure to include a summary slide with the three to five points you intend to convey. Follow up the presentation by sending participants a synopsis of key messages to reinforce learning.

- *Presentation delivery.* The way you present material can be as important as the material itself. If you speak in a monotone or an uninspiring way, the participants' minds will wander and they will lack engagement. Avoid being contrived, but make sure to convey an attitude that the material is important and needs to be communicated. Your enthusiasm in presenting the material to the audience can be infectious. When delivering a presentation, make sure to move your eyes continually between the computer projector and the audience. You don't need to turn around to look at the screen; you know what's there.

- *Pacing.* Most of us can experience some anxiousness when speaking publicly. Be conscious of slowing yourself down and make sure to breathe regularly. The presentation of each slide should take an average of three to four minutes if there is no audience interaction. You're not in a race to get through the material. If you know your material thoroughly, your confidence will rise and your delivery will reflect it.

PAPER PRESENTATION

Paper presentations are another common method of conveying information. Typically, you will use this method when you are seated in a round-table format along with the meeting participants, so it is easier to facilitate than when you stand and present. Paper presentations also allow meeting participants to write notes and have a reference document when they leave the room. For this reason, they are the most effective means of stimulating discussion. This format allows you to more easily follow up with participants and move the presentation content into actionable plans.

Paper presentations should be limited to two to three pages with well-spaced and well-organized information. Numbers, rather than bullets, are suggested so you can refer to a specific point and the audience can quickly identify it.

All the principles for the projection method apply in relation to key points being communicated, audience engagement, questioning of participants, and eye contact. However, the content and format should be more concise than in projections. Also, moving through the material at a slower pace will help you illustrate and reinforce key concepts. As with any kind of presentation, you need to know your material thoroughly, present with enthusiasm and confidence, and focus on the three to five key points you want to communicate.

WHITEBOARD, CHALKBOARD, OR FLIP CHART

Whiteboards, chalkboards, and flip charts are good presentation tools, but they are significantly different from projection and paper presentations. Because you must turn your back on the audience, different dynamics present themselves. These informal media are good for capturing ideas in a brainstorming session and they're best used when someone is acting as a facilitator.

Write the agenda and key items on the board or chart before the meeting begins so participants can see them and you can refer to them during the session. Be extremely conscious of engaging the audience continually because your back is frequently turned away from the group. This requires you to turn quickly back and forth to the audience to sustain their engagement. Clear and large printing is essential so participants can accurately follow the discussion in the meeting. Similar to projection presentations, the room environment has to be arranged in such a way that everyone can clearly see the tool. These sessions typically keep participants engaged as they are fast moving and the content is dynamic.

As in any meeting, expectation setting is important so that the key points are communicated effectively and understood by the group. In sessions like these, the material being covered is less important than the interaction, brainstorming, and problem-solution scenarios. Be sure to allow ten to fifteen minutes before the session concludes to summarize what was discussed.

Because these presentations can be very interactive and bring forth many ideas, your role is to encapsulate the ideas, prioritize the actions, and summarize the meeting, as well as to follow up with participants in electronic or paper format.

Quick Reference

Attention to detail will set you apart as a manager. This chapter covered ways to use and schedule your time as well as techniques for creating effective presentations and taking notes when others are presenting.

Time Management

- Your activities should always be tied to your key initiatives.
- You should always map out your plan for the next day before you leave work so you can begin executing tasks quickly the next morning.
- You should handle each piece of paper, message, e-mail, and voice mail once and file it so you can easily access it later.
- You need to spend 80 percent of your time on the most important 20 percent of tasks and plans.

Calendar Setting

- You need to make sure you have time designated to regularly evaluate progress on your mission, goals, and plans.
- Your priority tasks and actions have to make it onto your calendar or they will never be completed.

- At the beginning of each month, you should determine which objectives you must execute and make sure your calendar reflects this.
- You shouldn't wait until Monday to confirm your weekly calendar; it should be set by Friday of the previous week. You should always go into the week with a full calendar.

Note Taking

- You need to develop a personalized system to capture information, process it, and act on it.
- An important aspect of note taking is the value it communicates to the speaker.
- You should plan what you will need to do with the information before you begin taking notes.
- You should focus on capturing only words or concepts that will help you reconstruct the content later.

Presentations

- Your number one priority should be to convey your content in such a way that the audience can learn it, retain it, and apply it.
- You should focus the presentation on three to five key points. They should be stated in the introduction, reinforced in the body of the presentation, and summarized at the conclusion.
- If you present too much information too quickly, the audience is likely to shut down and you will have wasted both their time and yours.
- You can direct questions to the group as a whole and to individuals to ensure their engagement.
- Computer or overhead projector presentations allow you to make eye contact with the audience while delivering the information.
- You need to know your material thoroughly so you don't have to read it during the presentation. Slow yourself down and make sure to breathe regularly when you are making a presentation.

- Paper presentations should be limited to two to three pages of well-spaced and well-organized information.
- Whiteboard, chalkboard, and flip chart presentations are best used by a meeting facilitator bcause the user's back is frequently turned away from the group.

Epilogue

T HANK YOU FOR taking the time to read this book; I hope it was beneficial for you. My hope is that you are inspired and encouraged to lead your team, whatever that team may be. As leaders, we have all been entrusted with the responsibility to guide the most precious resource of all: *people.*

As mentioned throughout the book, take the time to develop relationships with people. The product of these relationships is personal satisfaction, results, and effective management. As a leader, you are required to sacrifice a tremendous amount, but there is no greater feeling than having guided a team to fulfill significant goals and having enjoyed the relationships you made on the journey.

Index

About the Author

D EAN SICKELS IS a professional manager who has held a variety of positions in the technology, education, and ministry fields. His passion is for his faith, family, and friends. Dean's experience in public and private education, start-up and large technology companies, and ministry have given him a unique perspective on how to effectively lead and manage people in a variety of fields. He resides in San Diego, California, with his wife, Sydney, and children, Erin, Kevin, and Robin. Dean dedicates significant time and energy to helping students develop the life skills necessary to pursue educational and economic opportunities for their futures.

About the Cultiver Group

THE CULTIVER GROUP specializes in equipping leaders and organizations in the twenty-first century. The company provides innovative content and training that cultivates outstanding leaders, grows organizational capacity, and produces exceptional results. Its mission statement is simple: When you execute on your mission, we execute on ours!

Managing People: Processes, Strategies, and Tools for Leaders and Managers in Every Field is meant as a best-practice reference guide. The book, along with other excellent content, has been translated into training materials and workshops for organizations in the private, public, and nonprofit sectors. These workshops are led by experienced managers who will bring applications-oriented training to your organization.

Training sessions and workshops can be arranged by contacting the Cultiver Group via its website at http://www.cultivergroup.com or by telephone at 760-730-3411.